BELIZE
BUSH TEA AND MUDDY WATERS

THE POETICAL WORKS
OF
F. DANIEL BRACKETT

BELIZE BUSH TEA AND MUDDY WATERS

A COLLECTION OF POEMS IN EIGHT BOOKS

Book One: BELIZEAN MEMORIES

Book Two: REFLECTIONS ON NATURE

Book Three: LOVE AND FRIENDSHIP

Book Four: BEYOND BELIZE

Book Five: WORK WOES AND WONDERS

Book Six: LAMENTATIONS

Book Seven: SPIRITUAL REFLECTIONS

Book Eight: ANTHOLOGY

Published by: Franklin Daniel Brackett
Website: Fdanielbrackett.com
Facebook: www.facebook.com/fdanielbrackett

With the collaboration of Jabiru Books Belize LLC

Website: http://jabirubooksbelize.com

First Edition Published 2022.
Copyright © 2021 Franklin Daniel Brackett, Coral Springs, Florida
Library of Congress Control Number: 2021925628

Deep Editing and Cover Design: Dr. Henry W. Anderson.
Print Layout, Formatting, and Typesetting: Stephanie D. Anderson and Dr.
        Henry W. Anderson, Jabiru Books Belize.
Printed Book and E-book conversion by BookBaby, U.S.A.

Printed Book ISBN: 978-1-09839-114-0
E-Book ISBN: 978-1-09839-115-7

Dedication

For Gwen Brackett,
My sweet mother, and
The first poet I knew

And
For Lu

"All the rivers run into the sea; yet the sea is not full; unto the place from whence the rivers come, thither they return again."

Ecclesiastes 1:7
The Bible - King James Version
(in Public Domain)

Acknowledgements:

Special thanks to Dr. Henry Anderson and his wife Stephanie of Jabiru Books Belize who facilitated the processing of the book for my self-publishing. Henry read and re-read the manuscript several times over and advised me along the way on how to perfect it; and our working together has made us into better friends.

Special thanks to my wife Lu Brackett who worked tirelessly typing and retyping the manuscript for this book. Lu was eager from the start, to aid me in every way possible.

I must say thanks also to my friend Jeremy Lemus of Santa Elena, Belize, who drove me around the Cayo District taking pictures for this book.

Thanks to Dr. Kwabena Amoh and Dr. Gayle Payne-Foreman who both read a cross section of the poems and gave valuable feedback.

Thanks also to Alejandro Perez and Anaceli Coyoc for sharing their Spanish language expertise.

Thanks to Mark and Lori Wukawitz for their continuous encouragement throughout the time I was writing this book.

Special thanks to Jewell Lewis who first suggested that I write.

Finally, thanks to my friend Joe Perez and all those who in some way or the other aided me, perhaps simply by asking about my progress in writing this book.

Biography of F Daniel Brackett

F. Daniel Brackett, my friend for over thirty years, is a poet and storyteller who grew up in a farming village in rural Belize and presently resides in the United States. Early in his life, Brackett began memorizing selections from the works of such Belizean poets as Leo Bradley and Ray Barrow; but he also recited poems from the works of British and American writers such as William Cowper, Robert Frost, Walt Whitman, and Langston Hughes among others.

Throughout high school, and while taking classes at the University of Minnesota, Brackett captivated audiences by reciting poems for them. He has spoken before thousands of people in several countries including Belize, Canada, the United

States and Mexico; at political public meetings and conventions, at schools and churches, and at youth rallies.

Besides reciting poems, giving speeches, and telling stories, Brackett delights in getting together with family and friends on special occasions, where humor and good food are appreciated. He enjoys fine dining which includes a porterhouse steak, but he wouldn't pass up a hot dog stand in Mexico, nor gravy on his fries when in Canada.

Drawing from his life experiences and fictionalizing them, Brackett has written many poems on a variety of topics. He has decided to publish a book of these poems, thereby sharing them with the world.

"Belize Bush Tea and Muddy Waters" is that book, and it offers a nostalgic interpretation of the complexities of Brackett's life growing up in a developing country with big dreams yet dealing with the difficult realities of everyday life. These poems are creative expressions of a storyteller whose vivid and descriptive anecdotes pull you into the moment as you read. F. Daniel Brackett has more stories to tell. This book is only the beginning.

Clarence Lindon Hulse

FOREWORD

I have known Brackett (as I have always addressed him) for several years, and during those years we have spent much time together discussing various topics especially those concerning our home countries. During small get-together meetings with our friends, I have always been fascinated by his recitals of various poems. *Belize Bush Tea and Muddy Waters*, the title of this book, refers first to "tea leaves" which Brackett's family, like many others who lived in rural Belize, often gathered from the Rain Forrest on early mornings and drew to make hot tea at breakfast time. Second, "Muddy Waters" refers to the flood waters of the Old River, the main source of water supply to the village. Upon reading these poems, one will clearly see that rivers played an important role in the Author's early life. His poems cover a broad spectrum of life situations.

For example, *To Belmopan* appears to be advising politicians in Belize, not to be selfish, but to be fair to the people, "let your eyes see as far as the Jankro saw, and your beak pick food not for yourself, but for both the needy and the strong".

The poem *To Robin (My Confession)* describes a lady who falls in love with a man, but he fails to reciprocate the love because he is afraid of engaging in a relationship. Later in life, the man apologized for the pain that he had inflicted on the lady. These two poems demonstrate the author's built-in sense of moral manifestation, and thoughtfulness. *Belize Bush Tea and Muddy Waters* reminds me of growing up in Ghana. The Author reflects on his childhood in Belize, when his mother used to prepare tea and hot Johnny Cakes for breakfast. Likewise, my mother used to prepare corn porridge with bread for me and my brothers.

I find Brackett's poem collection touching, and one cannot escape having a personal sense of similar experiences while reading through them. Some of these poems present constructive interpretations, while others can be funny. *Hired*, for example, presents a story between two men who are engaged in a dispute about ownership of an orange tree. The comical argument between them grew tense in the presence of a nine-year old boy who eventually became terrified and left the scene.

Brackett writes well, and he has a natural way of communicating with his audience. I personally recommend everyone to have a copy of *Belize Bush Tea and Muddy Waters*. You will enjoy reading these very worthwhile poems and will have varied adventures each time you read through them.

Kwabena Amoh, PhD
Former Adjunct Professor of High Education/Senior Academic Administrator
University of Cape Coast
Ghana

CONTENTS

Credits and Permissions
Photographs and Images

PHOTO	PAGE	PHOTOGRAPH
Author and Hawksworth Bridge, Belize	Front Cover	Jeremy Lemus
Author	Back Cover	Patti George
Author	Biography	Patti George
Mopan River, Belize	Book One	F. D. Brackett
The Roaring River Belize	Book Two	Ephraim Louis Usher
Hands	Book Three	Dhivehiraajje from Pixabay
Snow Covered Road-Northern Minnesota	Book Four	Anaceli Coyoc
Broom and Shovel	Book Five	Stanley H. Roberts Jr.
Cayo District, Belize	Book Six	F. D. Brackett
Ambergris Caye Belize	Book Seven	Joshua Elijah Brackett
Statue in Minnehaha Park, Minnesota	Book Eight	Stanley H. Roberts Jr.

BELIZE
BUSH TEA AND MUDDY WATERS

Bush Tea and Muddy Waters

B ush tea and muddy waters,
These are the things I remember,
When my mind takes me back,
Into childhood days,
And life on yonder banks
Of the Old River,
Where I went looking for tea leaves,
And stared down at that muddy river.

Early mornings found me,
Picking green leaves,
From branches of trees,
Among bushes that grew
Near the Teakettle S-curve,
And places just above the river.
There, I heard the noises of
Flood waters rushing by.

On rainy mornings,
Moisture hung in the air,
As I looked down at the river,
Flowing there.
The muddy waters overflowing her banks,

The rippling never stopped,
While the River flowed
Throughout my childhood years.

I was up at five o'clock, almost every morning,
When my sweet mother lit the fire,
On that old wooden hearth.
The red wood burned with pieces of sapodilla,
Like an eternal flame,
And soon the water was hot enough,
To pour upon the leaves I'd gathered.
And I watched the watercolor change.

Then tea was ready,
Hot Johnny Cakes baked,
Were taken off the fire,
And cut into halves,
Then put back together with butter,
And a slice of Kraft Cheese or Dutch,
Placed in between the halves.
Then I sat down to breakfast.

So it was, my day begun.
Even in the rainy seasons,
Life was filled with bush tea,
Amid showers of rain,
But moments of pleasure.
I remember,
The cups of bush tea sweetened with sugar,
Brown as the muddy waters of the Old River.

Now I can still taste the tea, see the muddy waters,
The things I still remember,
On days when,
My mind ponders my past,
And the adventures of the life,
I long ago left behind.
I see my sweet mother light the fire,
On that old wooden hearth.

BOOK ONE

BELIZEAN MEMORIES

POEMS

To My Belize

You're the sunshine on days,
When the seagulls fly,
Above the beautiful bay,
Where the blue waves soften and die.

You're the hot days in May,
When blossoms come upon the trees,
And little children play,
In the coolness of the breeze.

You're the melodious music played,
The songs our choirs sing,
The sounds our great sea makes,
As the seagulls flop their wings.

Old River Days

Dry weather days found my family,
Down by the Old River,
From midday to dusk,
We soaked, seemingly forever.

For the river was our life,
In the heat of hottest days
We sucked on cubes of ice,
Because that was our way.

And the moments,
Teemed with friendships,
The love of family,
That was our basic gift.

The water was ever so cool,
Like the moments we shared,
We had the Old River, needed no pool–
For that we didn't care.

On this day we are together again,
My cousins and I,
And with friends we are gathered,
Sharing wonderful memories, of the Old River days.

Dry Weather Days

Days of endless summers,
   Dry seasons
Ever coming,
Ever going,
And on each transit voyage,

They graced my childhood years.

Dry weather days,
Times to remember
Along the path of my life.
We village people live in summers,
Hot as the midday sun
When it bears down hard upon us.

The sun bears down upon a lad,
A dirty shirt upon his back,
Machete in hand,
But he finds coolness down by the River,
Moving day by day,
Gently drifting on its way.

Down by Ron D's farm,
From one dry season to another,
We villagers swim
In the Old River,
Before the sun goes down,
On each summer day.

Days of endless summers,
Dry seasons,
Ever coming,
Ever going,
And on each transit voyage,
They warmed my childhood soul.

Early Morning

The cover comes off my cold skin,
And I look up to see my mother.
She says that I must begin,
To wake my siblings.
So, I sit up in my bed,
On this quiet Monday morning,
And mother shakes my sleepy head,
One final time to get me going.

I pull my sisters' hair,
And elbow my brothers,
Then absorb their awful stares,
When they see me and not our mother.
But I quickly leave the room,
To follow the sweet smell of the fire,
As it burns and blazes, always early,
And sings like a cheerful choir.

Mother tells me that the tea is ready,
Then she pours me out a cup,
And she says, "Hold your hand steady,
Or you will make a muck;"
And so begins most of my childhood days,

For, not to sleep late,
Is my merry mother's way,
That is her children's fate.
Then I leave the house to do my chores,
And father tells me to feed the hogs,
To clean the hog pen floors,
And, oh the odors that strike this lad.
Thereafter, I carry drinking water,
From the hand pump to the kitchen,
But at the pump there is a fight,
Then laughter when another kid gets beaten.

Father feeds the chickens,
He picks up some eggs,
And I am suddenly stricken,
With an urge to go back to bed.
But my mother shouts: "Eight- Forty-Five!"
Before I could pillow my head.
I have fifteen minutes to make it to school,
Or I'll be dead.

Right then I heard the music,
And a familiar announcement on Radio Belize,
"This is The Hour of Decision!"
The Billy Graham Evangelistic Association's Program,
That was being aired.
It was a confirmation,
The time was 8:45 a.m. in Belize.
So quickly I ran to school,
And arrived there at 9 a.m. sharp.

A Who-You Bird

W ho you?" a voice called out to me,
    I wondered who had called.
I stared up at a Ceiba Tree,
Where the rain forest stood tall.

"Who are you?" I asked in turn,
I shouted into the wind.
I feared it was the voice of one long dead,
Perhaps, that of a long-lost-kin.

"Who you?" that voice called out again,
"And who are you?" I shouted.
The answer was that same "who you" refrain
So, I asked what it was he wanted.

A half dozen times, "Who you?" was repeated,
Five times I called back aloud.
At last, a feathered creature alighted,
And I saw a red eye, Who-You Bird.[1]

---

[1] The *Who-You* bird is the common Pauraque, *Nyctidromus albicollis*. During the dry-season, especially on moonlight nights, the *who-you* call is a familiar sound.

Mystery River

The river is going somewhere,
    Steadily flowing by,
She drifts on without fear,
Reflecting trees and sky.

Where is her big heart going?
Down to the open sea,
She'll wash a thousand landings,
And places I shall never see.

I've stood upon a bank of the river,
To watch her drift on by,
She made some sounds like music,
As she moved on by and by.

I know the waves upon the sea,
Upon the great big ocean,
But the river is a mystery to me,
Because she's always going somewhere–
Drifting wide and free.

Amnesia

N o never, ever, will my cousin John return,
Forty years gone from his country.
Precious moments burned,
And for him a new day dawned.

There is where he wants to be,
"The Tropical World", says he,
"Is not anymore for me."
Though there, he spent his childhood days.

Now his memory fails beyond belief,
He finds no fun reflections,
For memory's like a thief,
That brings with it contentions.

He once asked me if there were,
Any good things I could say,
Or stories tell,
About changes since he left that day.

So boldly I said,
"The country is developed now,
And brand-new houses stand
Where beds of foxtail grass, used to feed cows.

Where there were pastures wide,
Beyond the rushing river,
On the southern side,
The village is so much improved.

River boats are no more the norm,
And the river is quiet half the year,
Modern buildings replace barns,
Now, you'd want to be there."

If only he could see the place,
Forget the times when he lived across the river,
Poor folks and farmers who made haste
To work, to feed their family.

When life, like lice, was nothing,
And then a hurricane came,
He left, a man running,
Using his feet more than his brain.

Forty years now, gone forever.
He never looked back at the world,
Of the country that gave birth,
First to the little child, then the man.

Who leaves behind a great pearl?
Family and friends?
Falls for another world,
Now his life is edging towards the end.

All things are forgotten now,
An entire country, the history,
Family and friends.
Alas, a serious case of amnesia.

Jun
(In Memory of Benjamin Garbutt Jr.)

J un is still alive, I know,
  Dreams and memories tell me so,
And just like the old years before,
On and on our friendship goes.

Jun died to those who knew him not,
He died to some who knew him much,
They said he was a good, young man,
But now he's only dust or sand.

Dreaming of the days that used to be,
I hear Jun laugh and talk with me.
When I was sick, sad, or weak,
Jun always came his friend to see.

One day above all others,
We did a crime in school,
Jun got fifteen lashes, said they were a few,

Because he knew I'd get mine too.

Another day I often remember,
Teacher told Jun to name his brothers.
Jun made me laugh and teacher did the same.
We both heard him include his own name.

With these memories of him in me,
I cannot say he's dead, you see.
These days, we still are friends,
Despite the age so dark with life's curves and bends.

Yes! I know, I know so true,
And all of his friends would say this too.
He lives, Jun lives.
He lives in the hearts of those he knew.

On Wasting Time

I was wasting time in the country,
When I saw a rabbit hop,
Right out in front of me.
Back-feet high in the sky,
Its head up and shaking,
Not joking, not playing,
Not hopping for the sake of hopping,
Not wasting time in the country,
As we were nearing the 21st Century.

That rabbit wasn't squandering time like me.
He was running,
For his life,
For his future,
For a new era,
Not waiting for evil to befall him.
No claws or beak or bite,
Would catch up with that rabbit,
Not wasting time,
In open country.

To The Roaring River

Roaring River wash my feet,
Rushing on your way,
O'er valleys wide and deep,
Gliding by this sandy bay.

Each time I come to watch you flow,
We're like old friends who again meet,
And in your moving waters fast or slow,
I wash again my weary feet.

Sometimes I stand upon the sands,
And watch you move on by,
What lessons do you want to teach
When your waters go up high?

I think there're things that I must learn,
Roaring River when we meet,
Maybe today some dream is born,
As your rushing waters wash my feet.

Hired

O ld man Joseph hired me, a nine-year-old.
    I was to climb the orange tree,
As a reaper of the fruits,
But just as I began to climb,
What broke out was a dispute.
Farmer James shouted, "You brute!
That fruit tree is mine,
And that's the truth."
So, I halted where I stood,
Held my position,
And did what I could.
Called out for the old man, "Come! Come!"

Old man Joseph sat on a stool,
On one side of the creek,
He called farmer James a fool,
Then Joseph came to his feet.
James was his closest neighbor,
Lived on the other side of the creek.
James shouted, "You sucker!
Don't make that child into a thief."
So, the quarrel went on,
A half hour or more.
James drew closer to me,

And Joseph growled.

I moved away from that orange tree,
  stood fearless and firm,
Or so I figured.
James might be careless with words,
Old Man Joseph didn't seem bothered.
But I left in a hurry,
Having endured all I could bear.
I don't know how long they argued and hollered,
But many years have passed, since I ran away from there.

Late Night In PG Town

P. G. Town on a Saturday night,
  Up late on the beach
Where the sands are white,
There we'd planned to meet.

Three friends reunited,
With time to burn,
By the friendly sea,
We stayed 'til the windy morn.

I can't remember all we said,
Or the things we did,
But I held up my sleepy head,
And my weariness hid.

The time flew by,
Like the wind on the sea,
We laughed 'till we cried,
We were happy and free.

P. G. Town, up late that night,
Kate, Carmen and I,
On the beach by the light,
I can't remember what all we said.

Memories Of A Summer

I remember the summer of a year,
Or rather the dry season,
As now I think of yesteryears,
Of some people good and bad,
Of yonder places far away,
When I lived in Toledo.

It was a lonesome season there for me,
The pain of which I shan't forget,
Dusty roads, cold meat sandwiches,
And the smell of fresh manure,
In pastures where I roamed,
Singing songs in wildest tunes.

Yet, some things I now remember,
Like the waves of loneliness I felt,
As I gazed upon the greenest forest,
From those pasture lands I roamed,
Bring me no more of the sorrows,
That had torn my heart apart.

Tunes of that dry season,
Now bring me memories of some fun.
I think of guys like Kenneth, Otis, and Hamm.

Friends who tried to cheer me,
With their little music band,
And the everlasting folly,
Of some silly girls in town.

Cow Pen Days

C ow Pen Village farms spread out wide,
    Their corners, their edges,
Their sides.
The wages,
Not bad enough,
To make me run away from there,
As many other lads,
Under that southern sun,
Would've probably done,
When days were hot as fire,
The rain showers few,
And tenant farmers wanted to hire.

I took a job with Albino,
Spread fertilizer at banana tree roots,
The kind of work I used to dread,
The long days working in the morning sun,
And afternoons,
So very hot, and so very long.
And, oh the drops of sweat, like blood,

All Dry Season long.
There was little water for a time,
The deep drains were dry,
And no rain fell
To wet my dry and calloused hands.

When the first evening came,
And a day of work was done,
We workers ran,
To climb on board
The waiting trucks,
That took us back into town.
And the trucks arrived,
Then the unloading was done,
But I would not wait around,
Outside the liquor store,
While others gathered there,
To drink away their pay.

Night finally came,
And found me safe at home,
Having escaped the heat of the day
And the droning sounds
Of bulldozers on the farms,
And the fields where they worked,
From dawn
'Til the time to go home.
Then I would rest,
And eat a decent meal,
A most pleasant time,

In all the comfort I could find.

But the nights seemed short.
At the dawn of each day,
I made an early start,
For I'd decided to stay,
Maybe for another year,
No less but no more,
As the days were hard,
And my muscles were sore.
Each day after another
Came the thought, "I should've gotten out".
Yet, I stayed on the job,
Despite my doubts.

The days became longer,
With each setting sun.
The bananas grew taller,
The weeds slithered round,
But the fruits were shipped,
When they slipped through the tool,[2]
Before they were full,
And before the rains fell,
When deep drains flooded with water,
Swelled o'er the fields,
And some fruits would be swollen,
Then they would split open.
When the rains grew heavier,

---

[2] The tool is a banana caliper used to check if the fruit is ready for shipping.

Very heavy, at times,
Water rushed down the drains.
Some farmers prayed
Against the falling rains,
Which once they wanted
When the land was dry,
But bananas planted,
Might be infected,
If the fruit-flies came, and
When the rains stopped falling,
 the spraying began.

I worked for months, 'till the last day came,
Departed Cow Pen and the farms,
And the daily commute west.
Left Independence Village,
The place where I lived out my sadness,
Did work that had to be done.
But life has more meaning now,
Goes beyond the daily grind.
I was happy to be gone from Cow Pen,
On my way to my home in Cayo,
I left behind the good people, but the awful farms,
And the droning sounds of bulldozers.

The Right Honorable
(For Cousin Tally)

A Great Politian, the Right Honorable,
Prime Minister of Belize,
He was so very nice,
That he could set one's mind at ease.
He once engaged me in conversation,
While we walked side by side.
It was a funeral procession,
Down streets narrow and wide.
He said that he'd met me before,
And he remembered me well,
From those days when he went
Campaigning,
In the village Teakettle.
He remembered my family too,
And though there was little time,
He had a story to tell,
If I didn't mind.
So, I began in earnest to listen,
"*Man,*" said he, "*when I was young,*
I met quite a few tough men,
But none like your cousin Robert.
Robert had a temper,
Anger enough to crush Heaven and Earth;"

The Prime Minister had learned of that fact,
After Robert once heard him,
Teasing our uncle William.
"You tease my uncle again,"
The Prime Minister continued,
Stating that Robert declared,
"a gonna shoot off your head—and
He didn't mean my head;"
So, I laughed out loud,
Then took in some dust from Cemetery Road,
And I had to spit while laughing,
Cause I knew that Robert was proud.
Yes, Cousin Robert would've shot *it* clean off,
And left it bleeding, no joking.
So, The Right Honorable never teased our uncle again.

The Biggest Animal

The funniest thing I'd ever seen,
One Prime Minister of Belize, paid a visit
To the old man called Jamaican Jean,
Junior and I were witnesses to this–
As we were to many such occasions–
When the old man experienced a surprise,
Which he always greeted with exclamations,
And big, wide open eyes.

On this day in particular,
Junior, my childhood friend, approached me.
"Come, come, let's go see Jamaican Jean,"
Said he.
We found the old man just inside his house.
He was picking through a bowl of rice,
And seeing Junior and me, he prepared for the worse.
But he was not expecting the Prime Minister.

Junior was shouting: "Godfather!
Godfather, go get yourself ready,
And put on your best suit,"
But the old man only steadied himself,
"Junior," said he, "What is the matter?
Why you got to come frighten me?"

Then, I burst out with laughter,
At what was to be.

Junior was still shouting,
As he told the old man,
The Prime Minister would be visiting,
And Jamaican Jean needed to look better.
"Go, go, go Godfather," said he,
"You go put on that white shirt.
Dress up like B and me."
Then, at last, Jamaican Jean was alert.

The old man did not believe Junior's story.
His eyes revealed his doubt,
But Junior shouted: "Godfather, hurry!"
So Jamaican Jean put on the white shirt,
No time for the suit.
Then all three of us rushed into the front yard,
Just in time to see the Prime Minister,
Approaching with his bodyguard.

Jamaican Jean wore thick glasses, but could barely see,
And most of the time he didn't look through them
When he looked at Junior and me,
Or at any stranger, or foe, or friend.
So, on this day,
The Prime Minister called out, "Mr. Jean?"
And the old man said, "Yes. It is me.
You, come on down this way."

When at last they met,
Jamaican Jean was right up close to him,
Staring into the Prime Minister's face,
Then said he: "I was picking some rice.
But tell me, Sir, a who you are?
And do give me the truth cause,
A got a lying godson talking in my ear,
And he just told me that it's the Prime Minister of Belize."

Said the Prime Minister, "Yes, it's me, Mr. Jean."
But the old man got up closer into the Prime Minister's face,
Looking bewildered and mean.
Said he, spitting, "A why you here at my place?"
The Prime Minister laughed,
Backed up some and said: "My friend,
I was campaigning down the road,
And decided to come see you."

The old man being a foot shorter than the Prime Minister,
Looked up over his glasses and smiled.
He shook his head twice,
Then waited for a little while.
Then Jamaican Jean exclaimed: "Good God, my pal!
Junior was not lying at all.
Here stands the biggest *animal* in the country,
Right here in my front yard."

Junior and I began to laugh,
We knew that the old man often called people 'animal,'
But this was beyond the mark,

And we'd argued whether Jamaican Jean
Would address the Prime Minister as 'animal'.
The Prime Minister's face turned red.
His eyes rolled from Junior to me, then back to Jamaican Jean,
When he realized what the old man had said.

Baca Jesus

A lad still attending elementary school,
  I'll call him Brad,
But I should call him a fool,
Because he'd followed another lad and some friends,
Up the Western Highway,
To where the fisherman Parker kept honeybees,
And there they encountered the old man on a certain day,
And decided to tease.

The fisherman, Parker,
He specialized in catching the Baca-fish,[3]
But he also caught swordfish and sharks,
To fulfill customers' wish.
And it was said that old Parker,
He never failed to fill a list,
When it came to swordfish, sharks,
And the Baca-fish

---

[3] The baca-fish is a type of catfish that was common in the Belize Old
    River.

No other fisherman in the village would make a catch,
No matter how hard on some days they tried.
They stayed up late on the river and watched their lines,
But on most days, they missed the tide.
Then when morning came along,
Villagers were often disappointed,
Until Parker came selling,
Swordfish, Sharks and the Baca-fish.

On this particular day,
Brad and his friends approached the fisherman,
But they didn't want to buy fish,
Instead, this fellow, Brad, began to tease,
"Baca Jesus", he shouted,
"Baca-Baca, Baca-fish Jesus!"
The old fisherman was not much of a talker,
But he was no Jesus either.

Most of Brad's friends began running away,
And the dust on the road was rising,
When Brad looked back, he was stunned.
Baca-Jesus was fishing for him.
Parker's years in the military were paying off,
Cause he still knew how like a devil to run.
The first assault on Brad was with Parker's wooden staff,
It flew like a bullet from a 12-guage shotgun.

Then Brad began to slow down,
But the old man picked up more speed,
And he began gaining ground.

Parker moved like a man on steroids.
In less than a minute, the chase was done,
Then Parker was beating the lad in a rage,
And that was how Brad, the fool, realized,
One should not judge a man by his age.

A noise broke out again on the path,
Leading away from the old man's place.
Brad's friends were having a laugh,
And they had escaped the fisherman's wrath.
They stood some distance off,
Lest Parker decided to continue his chase,
For each kid had freaked out with fear,
Still, they had time to waste.

Years later, in Teakettle, this story was retold,
And it sounded like only a joke.
Some villagers never knew the old fisherman,
Nor the truth that the people spoke.
Old Parker has died and gone,
The lad named Brad grew up and moved away,
But it was a lesson some kids had to learn.
If you tease Baca-Jesus, you'll pray as you pay.

The Accuser

T he lad I called Jack, was one of my childhood friends,
   Like his little sister named Norma,
Both being Ms. Linda's grandchildren.
The girl was just a shy shorter than me,
At that time,
And Jack much taller,
Generous and kind,
If things were free, and
If he had something to share,
Like fruits or loot of a certain kind.
But what Jack could never bear,
Was a parrot with a brilliant mind.

Sad for my friend Jack,
Ms. Linda had a yellowhead,[4]
Bright, stubborn, and proud.
It remembered the words Jack's little sister said,
And it got loud,
Calling out the words,
The names of people, things, and places.
Then Jack called the parrot 'simple,'

---

[4] Refers to the Yellow-Headed Parrot, *Amazona oratrix*. Unfortunately, the population has decreased significantly in Belize where it is now illegal to catch them.

And that yellowhead began making faces.
I sensed there was to be a rumble,
Between the two, and that Jack would win,
But I was wrong.

Jack uncovered a cooking pot, still on the fire,
Extracted two pieces of meat soaked with gravy,
Not a lot,
Just enough for himself and me.
But that parrot went crazy,
Shouted: "Jack, you are sick!
You're a thief, you are lazy,
And you're full of nasty tricks;"
That parrot got louder,
Loud enough for the neighbors to hear.
That Jack would kill that parrot,
Became my greatest fear.

The two began shouting at each other,
"You just took two pieces of meat!" the parrot exclaimed,
"I swear I'll tell Grandma about everything you eat."
And so, the exchange of harsh words went on,
The shouting,
The quarrel.
And, oh, the things that I did learn about a bird,
That it can do much more than simply sing,
For that yellowhead could argue too,
Can threaten to bite,
Can fake an attack at you,
Can start a serious fight.

I stood still looking at that parrot,
Then at my friend Jack and at Ms. Linda's cooking pot,
That stood just below the ledge where that parrot sat.
Its head tilted to one side,
Its eye surveying Jack and me.
I observed its obvious pride,
And knew that the bird would not give up,
And, perhaps, there was to be a murder,
When at last the real fight erupted,
Between that yellow head and my friend Jack.
And yes, I was wrong.
Jack did not win!

Rip And Go

The soldiers whooped, "Rip and Go."
    His response: "The Hammer Of Death!"
Folks called him so,
For the battles he met
When as a soldier he fought,
In that horrendous war;
The British knew,
He was the bravest of all.

He sat in the shade
Of the big mango tree,
The comfort he got
Was easy to see,
And he watched the road
As the lorries passed,
With soldiers on board,
Whooping war-cries.

Loud were the yells,
When the trucks seemed a wall,
Rip and Go ope'd his mouth,
Returning the calls.
A mile away,
They could be heard.

In seasons dry, or rainy and wet,
T'was Rip and Go, The Hammer of Death.

This went on
For many a year,
Then Rip and Go retired at home,
But he had no fear.
He was hardened by life,
But softened by time,
He lost one fight,
And away he pined.

His days on earth came to a sudden end,
On a calm summer day,
While a light wind blew
Across the Western Highway.
But no one informed the British,
That "The Rip" was gone,
Not the Camp Commandant, nor a private,
But it didn't take years for them to learn.

Still the soldiers go by,
Pass that big mango tree,
They stand in honor
Whooping war-cries,
In the heat of the day
They drip with sweat,
They whoop, "Rip and Go!"
But no answer comes, from The Hammer of Death.

Daughters And Trouble

I once talked to a man who said,
Daughters are *trouble*,
Both before and after they wed,
There're boyfriends, and housework, and *trouble*.

I felt the words he spoke,
Long after I left his house,
I thought of them as a joke,
But then . . . Are daughters trouble?

The man who spoke had seven,
I have only one;
And to me my daughter is Joy;
Why **trouble**? I don't understand.

I will not play to anyone's fear
Or worry 'bout what may be,
The *trouble* he sees in his future,
Has nothing to do with me.

So as I walk from his house,
I think of that man and his words,
Of his seven daughters of *trouble*,
And how much I love this one daughter of mine.

Ron Dee

B ig and black,
Ron Dee stood less than six feet tall.
In fact,
Some villagers don't even recall,
That he lived up the Western Road,
Just beyond the Warrie-Head Creek,
Where trucks hauled loads of logs,
Most days of the week,
Then they dumped their loads,
Mahogany, cedar, bitter woods,
And the workers wore what looked like rags,
I watched them where they stood.

Ron Dee dealt with cattle and timber,
His land stretched from beyond the creek,
Back to the south bank of the Old River,
Then West until the next village it meets,
And in the dry season,
The place was lit with electric lights,
Crimson,
Yellow, blue, green, and white.
Some shone steadily and wide,
Others blinked,
They lit up that dark countryside,

When the sun said goodnight.
As a little child I stood on the hill,
Across from the Warrie-Head Bridge,
Below which the water stood almost still,
And if one didn't know,
He'd think that the water never runs,
Yet, it did for half the year,
Not in the hot, dry-weather sun,
But when the days were fair.
I stood up there,
Watched Ron Dee arrived at his gate,
His brand-new Ford pick-up truck shining,
The wheels seemed not to roll, but to skate.

Often, I didn't see the full person,
That was the big, black man,
But I saw just his head and a shoulder,
For he was seated, seldom did he stand,
Whenever I found the time,
To see the man.
Because he was always driving,
Cruising past my side of the road
Where he would slow down to wave,
Or to avoid a pothole
Or to gaze at the girls,
On the edges of the road.

The rumors were that he,
Ron Dee,
The big man,

Was not one any man could deride,
For Ron Dee didn't bow to anyone,
Though one often saw respect in his eyes,
Sometimes, disgust and defiance
For those who spread lies,
Often told under the Mango tree,
In the village, Teakettle.
Ron Dee believed some folks would never be free,
To live and simply to settle.

Some men will always be fine,
While wasting time,
Spreading rumors ever so subtle,
Possessing a will to make trouble;
But Ron Dee was second to no one,
And rumors had it further,
He was the richest black man on the Western Road,
From Cayo down to the City, Belize,
Where the timber logs were received,
At the end of drive-wood days,
And the log owners were always pleased,
In so many ways.

I never knew, would never know,
What trade made Ron Dee so rich,
Maybe more the cattle,
Yet maybe the logs,
But rich he certainly was,
And he was among the few,
Whose name was a persistent buzz,

Especially when he bought,
That new, blue, F-150 pick-up truck,
Clean as a whistle it was,
A sign that he had the big bucks,
And he had much more than a few.

Ron Dee owned houses in different places,
The colors of his houses etched in my memory,
Land in other villages,
And in many cases,
Places rich with timber,
Mostly cedar and mahogany.
The logs I remember most,
And the numbers
Stamped on the logs,
Before they were dumped into the Old River,
After being dragged
Through the pasture.

Many mornings did I stand there,
Evenings, by the Warrie-Head Bridge,
In the summer weather,
Up upon that ridge.
I watched the cowhands on cattle drives,
Listened to their voices loud and clear,
The noises,
And the stampedes which made me fear
That a cowhand would be killed
If something went wrong,
Like a bull's horns drilled,

Deep into the skull of a man.
But nothing went wrong,
Not one cow attacked,
That the men and monsters shared
An understanding, seemed a fact,
And I continued to look,
Day and night,
And saw the electric lights,
All along the way,
All lined up along the wires,
As far as my eyes could see,
Sometimes like torches of fire,
At times, a still persistent beam.

At events in the village,
Ron Dee was often seen,
All dressed up in blue,
Looking cool and clean.
Sometimes he was at the church,
The one on top of Cedar Hill,
Wearing his blue shirt,
As if it were God's will,
And they seated him up high, on the stage,
Which I found funny,
For Ron Dee was no saint, not even a preacher,
But he had enough money.

The mind of a child can figure out things,
His eyes ever ready to see,
His heartbeat rising,

In anticipation of what is to be,
But I never figured out anything,
And when, at last, the unexpected happened,
It was not my mind,
But my ears that started to ring,
The news was that Ron Dee had gone on to heaven,
And I was told of a fatal accident,
Informed that the new, Ford truck,
Was all crushed up, twisted, and bent,
Having been run over by a huge oil tanker.

"Good Heavens," was what my neighbors said,
The obvious shock showing on their faces,
Each shaking a saddened head,
As they went off to their places,
Some back toward the village center,
Others further up the road,
But I remember Ron Dee,
All over again,
Big, Black, and Rich,
He stood less than six feet tall,
And it is so sad, but indeed a fact,
That Ron Dee's name, few villagers can recall.

On Reaping Oranges

Under the shadows of the mountains towering blue,
The forest filled with flowering trees,
We sit staring up at the mountains,
In the early mornings,
Sleep still heavy on our eyes,
When we see the oranges,
The yellow fruits,
Waiting for us, The Rascal Reapers.

Early on weekend mornings,
This trip is taken,
Every time with someone
Who is hiring,
And we willing Rascals sign on
To reap, but we lads will eat,
Dozens of oranges in one sitting,
Under the shadows of the mountains towering blue.

Rows of orange trees in groves,
The orchards down by Roaring River,
Its water shines
And its golden rocks glitter
As the sun beats down,
Beaming on everything,

And on everyone who has come
To reap and to eat.

When the call comes, we start,
And each lad picks a row of trees,
Begins to perform his skillful art,
Of climbing and picking,
Bagging without ease,
Sometimes, among wasps and bees,
Or iguanas sunbathing on the limbs of the trees
Near bays of sands, the work begins.

We work, we reap, we drip with sweat,
Some days from six to six,
Sometimes, from sunup to sundown,
Until it's time to lift
The hundred-pound bags of oranges.
We load them on a truck with a regular bed,
Or one with sides of solid boards,
Built up high for the biggest loads.

Then there's little Rascal talk,
Little sound of laughter,
No shouting,
We work, we take on nature,
We fight prickles, branches, bees, and wasps,
For come the Tenth Day of September,[5]
We'd all have money to spend,

---

[5] Each year, on September 10th, Belize celebrates the anniversary of the
    Battle of St. George's Caye which took place in 1798.

Then we can buy new shirts, pants, and tennis shoes.

But the days are long.
The sun beams fire,
And water runs out as thirst begins.
Then the boss instructs two boys,
"Go down to the river,
fetch water for these Rascals."
The water arrives, our thirst is quenched,
And we return to work.

We slow and stop as the sun sinks
Behind the mountains towering blue,
And armpits, like skunks, do stink,
As we line up,
To await our pay, while -
With sharp eyes we watch the cheating boss,
For his habit is to miscount,
When he is calculating.

The day ends as it had begun,
Rascals climbing aboard the truck.
We sit on oranges, bounce over rocks, moving slowly,
But oranges begin to fly and boss brakes to stop.
We gather the fruits that fell to the road,
Great danger there, vehicles passing near,
But we Rascal Reapers have no fear,
We secure the load, then slowly move along.

On the way, folks offer to buy some fruits,
The Rascal Reapers work once more,
We fill their needs
Then board the truck again,
Still moving slowly,
Going home as we'd left each morning,
Sometimes feeling cheated,
Sometimes beaming.

We reach the village with the setting sun,
Each Rascal runs on home,
Cash in hand and ready for fun,
A chance to roam the empty village streets,
It's Saturday night,
And everyone is partying.
It's time for refreshing,
But the weekend's quickly disappearing.

A Beat For The Baymen

M orning is a Belizean sunrise,
    Rays penetrating the soul of a man,
My heart muses in the coolness of the moment,
The memory of our forefathers claiming their land.

Far away on the waters drifts my mind,
Where a thousand mornings came along,
Sunrises that found the bodies of Baymen soldiers,
Buried in the seashore sands.

Today I shan't forget the yesteryears,
When fighting Baymen gave their lives,
At Saint George's Caye, now a silent stand,
Still my mind muses at the result of it all.

Granny Mum-Mum

G ranny Mum-Mum stands six feet tall,
Taller than most any woman I've ever known,
Stands strong like an ancient wall,
And as rugged as ever she's been,
Through tough times, good times and bad,
She is the mighty pillar of my family,
Through tough times, good times and bad,
I thought she'd never be gone.

Hair long and white as wool,
Pulled down in a ponytail,
I see her truly full
Of the years that prevailed,
Or simply assailed,
Her life, her very being,
The good wife, the strong mother.
Yet now the years grow lean.

Granny Mum-Mum is,
The lifeblood of my family,
The constant strength,
Yet, with love, with grace, with all civility.
Then, suddenly, I got the news one day,
That my sweet Granny Mum-Mum was gone.

Moved on forever,
An era past, a new day born.

Now all that's left are the memories,
Stories told of when Granny Mum-Mum was young,
And stronger than any neighbor,
Always singing her favorite songs,
While biding her time.
Always the good, always the strong,
Awaiting the call as if from a glorious death,
For to her, Death is an Angel who makes right life's awful
wrongs.

The Old River

T he Old River is my life,
   It flows right by my home,
At times it floods the fields and pastures,
And places where I roam.

Sometimes, it's slow and gentle,
Sometimes, it's swift and strong,
It can get quite angry,
And do a few things wrong.

But this river brings me pleasure,
I'm swimming every day,

Its waters wet my weary feet,
And cool them as I play.

This River

This river runs right by my home,
    Five hundred yards away,
I visit her when I'm alone,
And in her stream, I weigh.
She's like a lonesome person,
Drifting down life's way,
Rippling, I see no reason,
Moving day by day.
Sometimes I sit and watch her,
Drifting down towards the sea,
I'm captured by her lore,
As she makes music for me.

The Epigram

Sweet sound of yesteryears,
    Sweet voice of my Grandmother,
Sweet love brought tears,
Each time my family gathered.

Sweet Home Of Mine, Teakettle

How peacefully now you stand,
　　Sweet home of mine, Teakettle,
As though your past were such,
That you've seen no trouble,
But you've seen so much.

I remember well my childhood days,
The ways of village folks,
Their parties went on all night,
And life was something bright
But often, fun lead to fighting.

The fights I shan't forget,
A knife, an ice pick,
A cut in someone's side.
I was just ten years old,
The fighting made me sick.

Gambling was in the culture,
Men rolled dice for big, big bills,
And that brought the biggest trouble,
Drunken men fought one another,
They pulled shotguns and fired.

When there was peace,
Chi-chi birds sang from the heads of bay-cedar trees,
Children walked to school in the midday sun,
And on The Tenth Day of September,
We marched like Baymen Warriors,
Proudly did I step-in-time and carried my own flag.

Though there were peaceful moments,
Change came again to you,
Sweet home of mine, Teakettle.
The fights returned,
And again, the guns were fired.

How many are your wounded children?
Minds scarred by the gambler, the drunk, the brawler.
Who can give an honest count?
I feel for those still living,
I feel for those long gone.

How peacefully now you stand,
Sweet home of mine, Teakettle,
As though your past were such,
That you've seen no trouble.
But you've seen so much.

You're My Belize

No country stands before you, my Belize,
Everywhere else is nothingness.
At most memorable moments I would leave,
The faraway places for you, the utmost best.

And when I'm far away from your comforts,
From the true joys of your open savannahs,
My heart yearns for a glimpse,
Of your cool, calm, cabanas.

Shadowed memories linger, sheltered,
Deep in the distant places of my mind.
I love you Belize, yonder land of flowers,
Amidst the roaring rivers of my time.

You're my Belize forever,
You're the wondrous voices of my childhood,
You're my love, my laughter,
You're my true home, the pure, the peaceful, the good.

On Visiting Belize

Belize! The hot sun!
Burning rays beaming through my bones,
But I was born here,
And once I loved this sun.

When I was a child,
And the days grew hot,
I lived for the windy evenings,
And awaited the cool nights.

But now on this visit,
I am sleepy at dusk,
Burned out from the day,
And barely enjoying the nights.

Still I don't sleep my time away,
I'm alone, but I'm still staying up late,
All set in my foreign ways.
This is something my Belizean friends hate.

To Belmopan

Oh Belmopan! Government and Politicians,
    You solidly stand upon a mountain top
Where once there were trees,
Upon which the jankro[6] sat.

Like the jankro, use your vision,
And among the people
Cause no crazy, political division.
Institutionalize no evil.

Let your eyes see,
As far as the jankro sees,
And your beak pick food, not just for yourselves,
But also for the poor, the needy, and the weak.

---

[6] *Jrankro* (var: *Jankro*) n. is Belize Kriol for 'John Crow', the Black Vulture, *Coragyps atratus*. It is a familiar sight over almost all of Belize, except the cayes.

My Sweet Teakettle

Teakettle Village sits,
   Overlooking the Old River,
She watches down upon it,
Flowing by forever.

Hills surround Teakettle Village,
Like Jerusalem, the City of God,
She's peaceful, protected, and privileged,
Here nature stands guard.

Green valleys are here,
Places where her children play,
Her men know not despair,
Her women are the sweetness of the day.

Teakettle will always be home,
Thought her sons may travel afar,
And her daughters follow,
Into the distant lands.

Yet, her children come full circle,
They return to their home,
And like the giant hills, they stay,

Each longing a void to fill.

Tonight, I long for home,
And should there be wealth in distant places,
Still give me back my home, my sweet Teakettle,
And all her familiar faces.

Oh, give me back the bygone days,
Cool moments in the Old River.
Give me back my village ways,
The joys that were to last forever.

Give me back my friends, my family,
The village where my father settled.
Take me back to live there happily,
Oh, give me back my sweet home, Teakettle.

Where I Lived

The old house stood by the road,
There, it no more stands,
For it fell under a burden,
Of vines, bushes, and sands.

The signs of life are there no more,
No limes, no lemons hang,
From trees planted near the doors,
Where the birds joyously sang.

I still remember that old house,
Sitting there alone,
Like my grandmother,
Each their own sorrow borne.

Now years after we'd moved away,
Father, mother and children,
I see the old house no more,
Yet, deep feelings remain.

Belizean Beaches

S eashore sands scattered on beaches,
　They're white with withered bones,
Where centuries of coral life lived,
And died upon these places I comb.

Seashore sands blown by the wind,
They dance in undulation.
So many beautiful beaches,
Inflame my imagination.

Seashore shines from sheets of sands.
These are glittering beaches!
Here extinct creatures lived,
Here their cry still reaches.

Seashore sands,
Blinding my eyes.
My lens adjusting,
before I see the shells.

On Some Summer Day

On some summer day, I'll find,
　　When the wind is willing to blow,
And I am of a sober mind,
The will to simply sow.

Maybe a few acres of corn,
Along the edges of my place,
Where for wondrous years my father farmed,
Before he left this life in haste.

Deep down along the dense part of the woods,
And where the bushes no longer grow,
I'll plant anything that can be good,
Upon which the wind might blow.

And many summers after this,
When the rains will have come and gone,
And farmers like me make their wish,
I'll spend a summer relaxing on my farm.

F. Daniel Brackett

Roaring Reef

Roaring is the Barrier Reef, it beckons to me,
The waves are white as rain o'er the Caribbean Sea.
The giant rocks,
Are washed with shock.
The sounds a sweet refrain.

I stand on this shore,
Here sands meet sea,
The waves are wild,
Not one is mild,
Am standing on Ambergris Caye.

Baymen Country

B aymen Country calls to me,
A son of her soil and swamps,
I hear the roaring of her Barrier Reef,
I see the glowworms fly.

Baymen Country calls to me,
Her voice is sure and sweet,
I hear the wind blow through the trees,
I feel her rivers wet my feet.

Baymen Country speaks to me,
Her voice is loud and clear,
Her people peaceful and free,
Her land is fertile and fair.

Baymen Country calls to her son,
Citizen of her land and sea,
And places where young turtles run,
On beaches white, as sands could be.

I call back to Baymen Country,
I speak to her on each new day,
From here in this, a distant Country,
Belize seems not far away.

Requiem For A Friend

U ntil a new sun rises in the east,
He who was my best friend sleeps,
Buried behind the family house,
Upon a nearby ridge.

For fifteen years, we ran together,
Played the games of a simple life,
And in the dry seasons,
Each day we kicked football.

After the games, Old River waited,
Rippling past that ridge,
And evenings found us soaking,
In her cooling stream.

We swam in the stillness of sunsets,
While shadows settled on village life.
Only then we'd climb the steep bank,
And parting, went on home.

During the dry seasons,
Endless mischief amused us.
When wrestling, Benji threw me every time,
But I always left him gasping.

At school we had our fun,
And studied for each test we failed,
Benji liked to provoke the girls,
I provoked the teachers best.

Then, one day, we were grown up,
Hardly mature, himself or me,
Still the evenings found us swimming,
And playing the games of that simple life.

One night as I slept,
At peace and deep at rest,
Someone called out my name, woke me, and said:
"Your friend is gone. Benji's dead."

God alone knows how much I mourned,
For the best friend I'd known.
Sadness, tears,
Have shaped me, in his silent years.

Each day I lived again my past,
I'd go to class and take more tests.
I'd play football, yet seldom did I score a goal.
 I seemed often to hear, Benji's familiar call.

Many years passed, I still swam in the Old River,
Just below that ridge,
Where the golden sun still sets,
On that place where my friend rests.

Deep inside, I do always mourn,
For the best friend I've ever known.
Be the brightest days, the darkest nights,
Be it sunrise or sunset on the village.

Twilights passed and gone, they come again.
Still deep inside, I shall always mourn,
For the best friend I've ever known.
Benjamin, buried by the river, upon a nearby ridge.

The Darkest Night

On the night that Benji died,
I hardly spoke a word.
Couldn't shed a tear,
For something died that night in me,
When I heard the news,
My Friend was gone.

I hurried down to the mortuary,
With whom?
I don't recall,
And there I found my Friend,
Lifeless,
Laid out on his back.

I saw him there in silence,
My voice unable to speak,
And at that moment in my life,
My world stood strangely still,
As did my childhood memories,
All taken away from me.

That night I sat up in my bed,
There was no effort to sleep,
Instead, I stared out of the window,
I'd lost Benji,
The friend of all my friends,
On that darkest night of all.

Letter To A Deceased Friend

M any years have passed,
So swiftly they went by,
Forever gone, forever lost,
Since Benji, that day you made me cry.

I remember how you were taken away,
In a coffin built so fine, like a Cadillac.
How gently there you lay,
Asleep upon your back.

The Villagers came out to see you off,
And all your friends were there.
We remembered how you made us laugh,
And we had so many stories to tell.

Teachers, preachers, statesmen, politicians, priest were there,
Your father's faithful friends,
Folks you would've come to know,
Each expressed regret and sorrow.

There were people everywhere, and oh the mourning in your
house.
Crowds upon crowds we stood, from road to river,
While still I held on to my doubt,
That you'd be leaving us forever.

Unwillingly, Benji, I said goodbye.

Mr. Blackhouse

Down in the village of Teakettle,
Down there, Mr. Blackhouse visited.
He walked around wearing black rubber boots,
While carrying an accordion.
I happened to be at a village dance,
As a lad back in the seventies,
When old Mr. Blackhouse was the musician,
Playing that black and white accordion.
The old fellow stood up straight,
And he started to play,
The time was about ten minutes to eight,
And I decided to stay for the night,
Though my mother must have been calling,
Not knowing where I'd gone,
I was caught up in the action,
And the music of the old man's accordion.

I found a seat and settled down,
While folks began to dance,
And a crowd of people gathered round,
Like those big marching army ants.
About that time, I heard somebody shout,
And I got out of his way,
Then the words came out of his big, loudmouth,

And he shouted: "Play, Mr. Blackhouse , play!"
The music picked up loud and clear,
As the musician reacted to that man's call,
I raised my voice, at first with timid fear,
But soon as loud as anyone on the dance hall,
And I shouted "Play, Mr. Blackhouse, play!"
Time was flying by so fast,
Some folks moved on and went away,
And a woman asked, how long can the old man last?

She must not have been from my village,
For everyone in Teakettle knew,
A Blackhouse Dance was an overnight affair
For those in attendance, be they many or few.
So, the crowd ignored the question,
And they shouted: "Play, Mr. Blackhouse, play!"
The music seemed to slow, but it picked up again,
And I moved back to clear the way,
Cause the old man nearly had a fall,
But he anchored those rubber boots to the floor.
Then again came that persistent call:
"Play, Mr. Blackhouse, play!"
The music was loud, but beautiful,
Mr. Blackhouse knew how to play.
He staggered a bit as he pushed and pulled,
And the crowd shouted again: "Play, Mr. Blackhouse, play!"

Midnight came and went.
The crowd began to thin out,
But the music flowed and flared,

As people continued to shout,
"Play, Mr. Blackhouse, play!"
And oh, the playing, and the dancing,
And the partying that was going on,
While the old man sweat and steamed.
The crowd continuing to shout:
"Play, Mr. Blackhouse, play!"
Then that accordion began to sing.
Leaving no doubt, it was Mr. Blackhouse playing.
Up and down he moved his body,
Side to side as he played that accordion.
He went down to his knees and hit the floor,
But Mr. Blackhouse was still pumping that accordion.

I shouted: "Play, Mr. Blackhouse, play!
Play, Mr. Blackhouse, play!"
You should've seen the young girls dancing,
As the old man played,
And oh, the swinging and the swaying.
The party was going to last all night.
No one then was checking the time,
They were going to dance 'till first light, or
Long as Mr. Blackhouse was playing that accordion.
Playing like a music machine,
Playing that black and white accordion,
Playing like a human machine.
About a quarter to five that morning,
Old Mr. Blackhouse went into a sitting position on the floor.
The music was now steady, but slow,
And the people shouted: "Play, Mr. Blackhouse, play!"

Outside the building where the dance was taking place,
Day was a breaking fast,
But the old man picked up the pace,
Determined to last 'till first light.
The roosters were crowing in the distance,
Flocks of parrots squawked in the trees,
More people left the building,
While others kept dancing away.
Mr. Blackhouse hit the floor on his back,
And all of us shouted:
"Play, Mr. Blackhouse, play!"
"Play, Mr. Blackhouse, play!"
It was daylight outside when the music stopped.
That accordion made a long and mournful sound,
That was the way Mr. Blackhouse wrapped it up,
And applause came from all around.

Some years later, I heard it said,
Down at a village bar,
That old Mr. Blackhouse lead
A long and lonesome life, and
That the only companion he ever had,
And the only friend he knew,
Was that black and white accordion,
The one he played that night.
It was the last time that I heard
Mr. Blackhouse play his accordion.
He made the villagers proud,
That one-of-a-kind musician.

And long after I left Teakettle village,
The music was still playing in my head,
Even today, I still hum the tunes,
And I whisper, "Play, Mr. Blackhouse, play!"

Old Mr. Blackhouse,
Teakettle's most celebrated musician.

A Tribute To Horace Ness
(For Emogene)

Horace Ness, more than an ordinary man was he,
Horace saw what few villagers could see.
He was not rich,
But a grocer with a rare sales pitch.

At his store, I came to know,
Horace Ness, no *papisho*;[7]
We children teased him, on and off,
And we listened to his scolding talk.

Village children gathered,
Even teenagers bothered,
We listened to his wisest words,
Of things we seldom heard.

---

[7] *Papisho* is Belize Kriol for 'acting stupid or foolish'. It is probably from
the Scottish "pappy-show, puppet show'.

He showed me how to till the soil and plant,
Taught me not to say I can't,
And I grew fields of corn,
According to the way I'd learnt.

Then Horace went slowly blind,
And in his home awaited his time.
Still he worked in his grey grocery store,
Selling salt-fish with his rare sales pitch.

When he died,
I was long gone from the village,
But on that day, he was honored
And rightly called the best.

A wheelwright from a Caribbean island,
In my village he settled,
The wisest man who ever lived in Teakettle,
The Great Horace Ness.

A Western Gentleman

B ill is a Western gentleman,
He wears an Al Capone hat,
He's proud of his heritage,
And he says he's from very good stock.

Bill is a Western gentleman,
Lived in Cayo District, Belize,
Where proud farmers run cattle and sweat among the furrows,
Hoeing, sowing, and reaping seeds.

Bill is a Western gentleman,
Sometimes, he's as humble as any farmer could be,
But don't mess with that Western gentleman,
Cause fire can blaze up from humility.

Bettie Jean

A hot summer day in dry weather,
I'm in Belize,
Walking the streets of Belmopan,
Sweat seeping through my clothing,
Pouring down my neck,
Until I seek the shade.

My American mind pretends
I'm having fun,
But the sun is brutal,
On these dry weather days.
I long,
For the unfailing coolness of night.

Six p.m. finds me ready to leave the city,
And Arnold takes the wheel
Of the little conversion van.
Cruises us down or up the road,
Into a small, darkened village,
Where we believe we're answering God's call.

At seven, the service begins,
And old man Berry shakes my hand,
While Jesse sings a song,

That touches everyone.
So sweetly my senses respond,
And my heart pounds my chest.

The next two hours grow,
From outset to zenith,
Then the service ends,
With one final tuning
Of Jesse Graham's guitar.
Then a song, and we all say "Amen!"

Arnold and I came to Belize,
Newly converted souls,
We found the life which once we'd lost,
In the days of old.
A chance to gain God's Heaven,
And the good that's left in stow.

It's time to leave the village,
And we say good-bye to all,
The humble converted villagers.
They made a house a sanctuary.
I, Bettie Jean, thank God I'm saved.
I am a missionary.

Sister Cathy

C reole bread baked on wooden hearth,
  Made ready for Sister Cathy,
The missionary.
She inspires everyone.
She shares God's Love,
And Love runs over.

Belize and its Teakettle Village,
Took a liking to her,
Down there she travelled,
And, oh, what Spirit! She bore,
Good tidings
Of life everlasting.

Sometimes the bread was gone,
But fry jacks would always do,
At dusk or at dawn,
They'd have food ready for Sister Cathy.
A surprise from the poor,
To her they opened their doors.

Time came to depart,
She must leave the village behind,
And, oh, the saddened hearts,
No hugs could fully express,

The deep distress,
When Sister Cathy was leaving.

The Liar

As a child of nine years old or so,
My mother kept her eyes on me.
I asked her what she knew,
What did she see?
What would my future be?
That made her begin to talk,
Hold conversations with me,
While we walked,
Up and down in our yard.
She asked me questions,
Advised me not to play with cards,
For that might lead me in a wrong direction,
When I grew up.
And she asked that I tell no lies,
But be truthful, gentle and kind,
So, I enquired, "Why no lies?"

"Son," said she, "a man must be discreet,
Know that a liar,
Is also a thief,
And a thief is a murderer.
Liars, thieves, and murderers,

Will all end up in prison,
And you'd rather not,
Give the law a reason,
To put you away,
To spend your life in a cell,
All through the nights and through the days,
Year after year."
Yet, I told a big fat lie,
Saved my backside from the whip,
But as time went by, I made a promise to my Sweet Mother,
The lying I would quit.

I'd never, never,
Tell a lie again,
Not ever,
While I travel down life's winding road.
And since then, but for a little white lie
Told here and there,
I'd not ever told a big, fat one,
To ignite my greatest fear,
That my Sweet Mother in her tomb,
Would somehow feel regret,
That she'd carried me in her womb,
Thinking that my promise to her was never kept.
For now, in peace, gently she sleeps,
While still in life I journey by and by,
The past and future might meet.
In truth, these days I never tell a big, fat lie.

On Leaving Teakettle

A subtle silence settled
    On the village,
In places where I roamed,
When I was coming of age,
And in my childhood years.
Memories flashed before my eyes,
In the noises of midday,
Last reflections before my departure.

I left Teakettle behind,
But I reminisce and the village is alive,
Children playing among the trees,
Cattle nibbling on the dry, brown grass,
Horses galloping on the range,
A neighbor sneezes.
The bus pulled away,
And the village was silent again.

I was moving on, yet
Looking back into the past.
The road ahead was eastward bent,
I was going astray,
Just a rearward look at my village,
In the heat of that dry-weather day.

My heart was weeping,
'Cause I was leaving my home behind.

My childhood days came back to me,
The memory of my parents too,
Young as they were in yesteryears.
My siblings congregated
As they played in shallow streams,
Animated,
And drenched in muddy water,
Down by the Old River.

My past is like my present life,
Both like a dream,
And when I had to leave Teakettle,
I knew I'd be missing her very soon.
For home is where the heart belongs,
Though oft' one must move on.
And time will travel along,
But ol' days will come to mind.

It's been ten years now, I went astray,
Ten long years ago.
Exactly ten years today,
And that's one fact I know.
I rivet my eyes, reignite my imagination.
Another look back at my village,
My sweet home, Teakettle.
I wonder what my future holds.

Fallen Hero

Father!
 You were my measure of a man,
And like you I live my life,
Striving for peace,
While avoiding life's daily strife.

I measured you as with a soldier's rule,
But you were greater than any soldier,
For when others offended you,
You kept your cool,
And your love never faltered.

All the while,
I looked on,
With eyes of admiration,
Even when you grew alone,
In silent desperation.

But from moments of confusion,
You turned and became stronger.
You nurtured me,
And gave me attention.
Father, you were my measure of a man.

Today I mourn for you,
My greatest loss.
You left me suddenly,
And I still wonder,
Why were you taken so soon?

Father, you're my Fallen Hero,
Struck down at the height of your life,
The true measure of a man,
And the wisest,
Greatest Father of all.

Celebration
(For Frank D.)

L ate night up in the sand bar,
     We sat there on bar stools talking.
Hillard, Curzon the poet, and I.
We sipped from glasses of
Alcohol beverages.
The moonlight bouncing off the waters,
Of the Caribbean Sea,
Found its way inside the bar.
Outside, the waves washed
Beaches of white sands,
At *Captain Morgan's Retreat*,
Down on Ambergris Caye.

The three of us had things to discuss,
Well at least two things,
Hillard and Curzon liked hard drinks,
But I always went with wine.
We swallowed the drinks,
While we talked theology,
And swapped lines of poetry.
One held a degree in religious studies,
And the other had wanted to be a priest.
I wanted to know,
What answers they could give,
To my questions about theology.

Our nights were long in the sand bar,
Good times the poet shared,
In conversation with Hillard and me,
While seawater was
Splashing against the outer edges
Of the pier. The sounds,
Punctuated the rhythms
In the lines of
Poetry we shared.
And glasses knocked in toast to one another,
Light libations,
Taken in celebration of the moment.

Curzon almost became a priest,
Hillard a minister.
But that was years before we met,

And they still remember their early dreams,
As now I do recall,
Stories told,
And promises made,
To one another.
Curzon promised to send us his book,
Hillard promised to keep in touch,
While he emptied the last drops from a bottle
Into Curzon's glass.

I promised to write,
To read up on theology,
And to read Curzon's poetry,
When he sent me his book–
"Trinergy."
Promises made,
Over drinks!
I can never recall the kind they had,
But I was no heavy drinker.
A listener–Yes,
And a talker,
Thrilled to be in good company.

The nights flew by,
And Curzon's time on the caye,
Came to an end,
Climaxed in one final night when we talked theology,
Before the poet said good-bye.
And I watched him step out of the bar,
Into the dimness of the outdoor lights,

Coconut palm tree- heads waving in the wind,
Then I saw him no more.
No, not ever again,
But Hillard and I still stayed up,
Late into nights talking theology and swapping lines of poetry.

Days drifted by,
They turned into weeks and weeks into months,
While Hillard and I waited,
Listened for news of Curzon.
Then surprise came in the mail.
We each got a signed copy,
Of the book called "Trinergy".
At Curzon's work, we'd take a look.
In school I had come to like poetry,
The writings of
Bradley,
Barrow, and Fuller.

Those Belizean poets,
Their writing kept me out of certain troubles,
And got me into others,
Because I knew how to quote them to the girls.
These days, I quote Curzon, Frost,
 Longfellow,
Shakespeare,
And a half-dozen others.
In winter times or in summers bright,
Early on weekend mornings,
Late into nights,

I read I quote.

It's been two decades since,
Hillard, Curzon, and I swapped poetic lines,
Up in the sand bar.
Decades since I left Ambergris Caye,
But still I read Curzon,
And still I think of Hillard.
I hear their voices in my ears,
The waves of seawater against the pier,
Those washing the white beaches
Of the caye and its little town,
San Pedro,
And the resorts up the northern coast.

Just the other day,
I enquired about Hillard,
Then I tried to find Curzon,
While wishing I was still on Ambergris Caye.
But someone told me that Curzon's book was out of print,
And Hillard lives no more on the caye,
At the place where we had met.
The years have gone by,
Ever so quickly,
Since those sweet, summer nights,
When we stayed up late talking theology,
And swapped lines of poetry.

Hillard and I

S an Pedro Town, when I was young
   And coming of age,
On beaches long,
Life reached a certain stage.

It was total fun,
Back in my day,
Years lived and done,
And perhaps thrown away.

Late up in the sand bar at night,
We talked theology and,
Under dimmed lights,
We shared poetry.

Hillard liked T. S. Elliot,
But I, F. Daniel, quoted Ray Barrow,
And this went on 'till sun was almost up,
With seawater whipping.

Each opened his book, "Trinergy",
A surprise from the poet,
He had not forgotten,
At Curzon's work we looked.

One book signed to Hillard,
The other to me,
One great poet to thank,
His words, good reading would be.

Thanks to the time
Curzon spent on the caye,
When the weather was fine,
And we swapped lines of poetry.

But Curzon went home,
Left Hillard and me alone,
Then came my greatest test,
And I too left to go home.

One final night up in the sand bar,
We talked theology,
While hurricane winds whipped,
With seawater and poetry.

How long? I can hardly remember.
Not long ago, I tried to find Hillard,
But someone told me he had left the caye,
Maybe, sometime late in last November.

Listening

Granny Mum-Mum once told me,
That Grandpa Bill never lived long,
And only a short, simple life had he,
A man, big and strong.

Thirty-nine years he toiled,
He worked his little farm,
Found a fertile field,
In which he planted corn.

Granny Mum-Mum stood,
Half those years by him,
She cooked, she cleaned, she burned the wood,
She cut the grass; the hedges trimmed.

"No" said she, "Your Grandpa Bill never lived long,
But, Grandson, I hope you live to be like him,
So big and so strong.
And may God give you a long life."

I sat in the kitchen listening,
Leaned back on the old rocking chair.
The whole talk was so enriching, and
Filled with Granny Mum-Mum's enduring love.

A Tribute To Gwen

M aud Gwendolyn!
Mother of many children,
They're now men and women,
People of different, distinct ways.
Thirteen grown children,
Thirteen miracle births!
Birthdays were times without end,
So often we celebrated them.

Maud Gwendolyn!
Mother of mine.
You are Heaven's child,
Now in Everlasting Time,
With no boisterous children,
As when you were on Earth,
Working through life's stages,
A mother giving birth.

Maud Gwendolyn!
I look back at your life,
The times that were my childhood years.
I hear your rollicking children,
I feel your ails and pains.
I see sadness in your eyes,

Yet I hear laughter in your voice.
You bore the sadness but lived the joys.

Maud Gwendolyn!
You taught your children to be strong,
Of love and hate,
That love is better,
And to obey the law down to the letter.
You taught us that we can do good,
Can live a life that matters,
Even though life offered you so little pleasure.

Maud Gwendolyn, gone forever.
You still are the joys of my life,
The one truth that truly matters.
You worked long days and nights,
You prepared the stews, the salads, the beans, the rice.
You cleaned the house; washed the dirty clothes,
And how you did it all,
Only the Almighty God knows.

A Tribute To Bill

William Benjamin!
Family man.
You walked the streets of this village,
Tall and strong.
Of how handsome you were,
The women used to speak,
And when you walked the streets,
You were strong, yet meek.

You donned your Al Capone hat,
Held your head high.
A man of strength,
I knew no other as strong,
No man with your style, your way.
You chose to do right, instead of wrong,
All under that hat,
Where you carried a smile.

For your family,
You were always there,
That hat on your head,
That smile on your face,
Most always in the same place, at home,
Those are the things, I remember most.

William Benjamin,
Family man.

Tall, handsome, and strong,
I hope you're happy in your new home.
Your departure was swift,
Unexpected, incomprehensible to me,
Cause you were physically fit.
So strong, and,
So proud of your name.
So proud of your name.

William Benjamin, man of strength,
I've spoken at length.
No unusual wisdom shared.
No special line of thought,
Just enough words to allay my fear,
That folks might forget you, Father of mine.
You cherished the night, but you loved the day,
And you lived your life, in your own simple way.

On The Death Of A Friend

How awful are the solemn songs,
That village people sing,
At funerals, at wakes,
But I long to hear them now.
Janell has died.

Janell!
My friend throughout my childhood years,
She solemnly swore to live,
A life pleasing to God,
And a lifetime of friendship with me.

For forty years we walked together,
Tall among the trees of Teakettle Village,
I can still hear her laughter,
While on life's road we travelled,
And I still feel the affection.

We were ordinary people,
Extraordinary friends.
We talked late into nights,
Clear with the moon shining bright,
Though there were times of dissention.

Still Janell was the best defender,
Against all my detractors.
What bad in me they saw,
Convicted me not, in the court of her opinion.
Oh Janell, my dearest friend!

I miss you so much today.
For you, I say a prayer.
For you there's God's Glorious Heaven,
A better place than here,
And there your happiness will never end.

Aunt Thay
(For Cousin Jenny)

Aunt Thay stood strong,
   Ready to confront,
Yet those she loved,
Were always right.
But those whom she hated,
Were always wrong,
And bad in her sight.
They would be distraught,
When Aunt Thay decided,
She would pick a fight.

Aunt Thay never forgot anyone
Who crossed her path:

The Good, the Graceful,
The Generous folk,
Those with an open mind and a good heart,
Sweet enough to befriend her.
She always tried to be strong,
For herself and her family,
And at the age of fifty, as in her youth,
She can still give any man a bad beating.

Aunt Thay told me once,
That she never feared men.
No, not their stance, not their prance,
No, not their hellish ways,
That make them go to war,
And beat up on innocent people.
On women who poured out love,
But got hate in return,
In painful moments,
incidents of abuse.

"No! They wouldn't dare beat me!"
That's what my Aunt Thay said,
As she shook her defiant head,
Relating her stories to me.
The things she did in her youth,
The stories I loved to hear,
And was happy to know,
About when Aunt Thay was young.
She was not afraid of anyone.
My Aunt Thay stood strong.

Great Spirits

W here are you Great Maya?
    You who ruled this land
And left it holding secrets,
In temples built by your own calloused hands.

Where are you Great Maya?
Builders of these temples high,
Sacred, hallowed wonders,
That astonish the modern eye.

Where are you Great Maya?
Children of Marcus Canul,[8]
Descendants of my hero warriors,
Maya kings asleep in sacred tombs.

Were you to answer me, Great Maya,
I know what you would say,
That Europeans came by land and sea,
And brought terror here one day.

---

[8] Marcus Canul was one of the better-known leaders of the Icaiche Maya.
The Icaiche Maya territory included part of northwestern Belize and
southern Mexico close to the Rio Hondo.

And terror would not cease,
Till the Maya almost saw defeat.

Horror, murder, diseases,
Still, you did not retreat.

Now where are you, Great Maya?
Silent heroes of this land.
Your temples are still soaring high,
In them you make your lasting stance.

Deluge

Rain is falling all around,
The droplets jumping off the ground,
The wind is angry with the rain,
It gusts, it blows the rain along.

I hear the rain upon my roof,
The beating never stops.
The wind and rain will make no truce,
In spate a river everywhere.

Rapids flow outside my door,
From the roof top, waters pour,
And swirl around my bush tea plants,
The angry wind is back again.

I huddle down inside my house,
The storm is getting ever worse,
Then water swirl and rush away,
I'll see a nasty flood today.

Roaring River

Roaring is the river,
Drifting on its way,
Rushing by forever,
In my childhood day.

Its water cool and comforting,
Agates much glittering.
I fish into evenings late,
With sunsets dazzling.

Some nights I sleep upon its bank,
The roaring never stops,
And though the jungle is ever near,
I sleep soundly, without care.

Roaring is the river,
Drifting on its way,
Its waters beckoning,
Even in my dreams today.

A Plate Of Boil-up

What wouldn't I do today,
   Or give,
For a piece of soup yam
Slowly boiled,
Belizean style,
Mashed up like Irish potatoes,
With salt-fish,
Cooked in virgin cohune oil?

What wouldn't I do today,
Or give,
For the foods I used to eat:
Sweet potatoes, cassavas,
Young bananas,
Ripe plantains,
Mauve yampi yams,
And a piece of game meat?

What wouldn't I do today, or give,
For a plate of Belizean Boil-up
Like Aunt Thay used to make.
The foods I used to love,
All cooked up together,
And seasoned to taste?

I'd do or give almost anything today,
For a plate of Belizean boil-up.

The Builder

When I was twelve,
    I worked with men,
Upon the houses high,
That was a time,
When life was fine,
And nothing made me cry.

The days were long,
We men were strong.
With pride we stood,
Working the mahogany wood,
With strength we built,
As if to touch the sky.

Then ten and two,
Now fifty and few,
Still I toil on and on.
I am a man,
Doing all I can,
But those youthful days are gone.

To The Old River

F looded river swiftly flowing,
   Through my childhood years,
To you much happy times I owe,
A life of joy and tears.

Two adolescent children died,
Paddling their canoe,
Your flooded waters stifled their cries,
I feared I would drown too.

But that time is passed,
Like lives in your flood waters lost,
Those two children are forgotten,
And my fears have lessened.

These days, I swim like a crazy man,
In the hottest times of dry seasons,
My best friends along,
For the obvious reasons.

Am just past twenty today, Old River,
Again, you afflict my soul.
I found a young man, perhaps my age,
Drowned in your flooded hole.

Flooded river swiftly flowing,
Through my childhood years,
To you much happy times I owe,
A life of joy, yet tears.

Wild River

T his wild river has a will,
   It's rushing through the Rain Forest.
I'm fishing in the middle of the stream,
And I don't know what to do.
I'm standing in the river with friends,
Big Birthy on my right,
His godson on my left.
Big Birthy shouts: "Flash flood!"
His godson shouts: "No!"
My fear overtakes my youthful pride,
 I see huge Mountain Cows.
They're in the water, coming straight at me.

The river is rising, the cows are coming,
Their heads raised above the water, high.
They're coming right at me,
And I think I'm about to die.
I pull up my fishing line,
Almost too late,

And it comes to mind that,
I'm wasting my bait.
The cows are drawing closer,
Loudly godson prays a prayer,
Then a strong hand pulls me away,
Increasing my fear.

One cow kicks water out my way,
Water splashes above my head.
It's a bad start to a beautiful day,
A deafening noise, and I smell the lead.
Shots are fired,
From Birthy's shotgun, one, two, three.
The third shot hits the first mountain cow,
And Birthy's 16-gauge, shotgun comes down.
All three cows take a downward bow,
Downstream they go.
Downstream through the forest green,
In the middle of this river, wild and mean.

On the south bank of the river,
Godson is praying still,
He's shouting for Big Birthy,
While attempting to run up the hill.
But the whole commotion
Is quickly over and done.
Peaceful is this wild river now,
As it was when the fishing trip began,
And before downriver came those mountain cows.
This wild river has a will,

It goes from a rage back to a peaceful still,
And now it's as silent as the nearby hill.

Grevenio

G revenio!
   For decades you stayed on my mind,
Since our childhood encounter,
During that stretch of summertime,
In that coastal hospital,
Where we lay across from each other,
Our beds set side by side,
And on each the toys we gathered,
Near windows opened wide,
And on certain days, the trade winds blew,
Past the veranda,
Which ran north and south,
And served as a corridor.
There like scouts,
The hospital staff went up and down,
The nurses at their best,
Moved around,
Well dressed.
The orderlies held their ground,
They did the heavy work,
Always rolling wheelchairs past our ward,
And from work they never shirked,

Even when it was hard labor,
And the days were hot.

Grevenio!
You held on to your fractured foot
As I on to my hand.
Imagine now the sorry look,
For we were both so sick,
Each with a limb in plaster,
Each only time would fix,
With the help of doctors,
None of whom I can remember.
No, not a single name,
No, not one face can I recall,
Not ever,
As prior to that time was my accidental fall,
And the long trip thereafter,
Left me confused,
And rather weary,
Bereft of joy,
Of laughter.
When I arrived at the hospital,
I found I would not be alone,
At least, not for long,
As we would both be staying in–
Another reason to mourn.

Grevenio!
I can hardly remember my pain,
For it's the memory of yours that I carry.

'What crying shame,'
It increased my daily worry,
And what mental strain,
That nobody could've helped a sick child.
For much of the time,
You were totally wild,
And seemed to be going out of your mind.
And oh, that screaming voice of yours.
It'll not be forgotten,
How you fought tooth and nail,
Whenever a nurse brought your medicine,
Or whenever you saw a needle.
For the thing we both always feared
Was the needle.
A shot seemed a great evil!
Yet, while I took mine in silent fear,
You screamed every time,
And we came to dislike the nurses.
I almost hated them deep in my mind,
Beneath my breath I whispered curses,
What insults I was able to find.

Grevenio!
Back then I knew I'd never forget you,
No, never, not ever,
Were I to live a thousand years on earth,
Or just another awful day.
For what else is friendship worth,
If I could not have wished for you,
As for myself,

A normal life?
One without pain and fear,
And filled with all things bright,
Throughout the days and nights,
A world without care,
A future in which you'd never have to suffer,
And in painful anguish shout,
But be awakened,
On each new day,
Not frightened or shaken,
But healthy and singing,
The songs that little children like to sing.
For such are the things
For which we longed,
When our pain was too deep to bear,
And we were not very strong.

Grevenio!
At long last, the day came when I ran away,
Tiptoed past the sleepy guard at the hospital gate.
Left in search of my parents,
And help for you, Grevenio.
I'd left while you slept,
Yet an unlucky child I was to be,
That certain fate I met.
For quickly the nurses missed me,
Then they guessed,
That the little country lad had escaped,
Still wearing the hospital gown,
And was gone down the street,

Passed the stores, the curve,
On swiftly moving feet,
Where curious folks would search for words,
And asked questions,
There where the orderlies caught up with me,
And I was remanded into that miserable world,
Of the hospital staff and their patients.
The doctors observing us all,
We, the unfortunate children,
And I never would escape your voice
Echoing through the ward.

Grevenio!
Our parents arrived.
At last, a moment of hope,
And a half day of rejoicing,
Filled with joy,
With gifts like chocolates and sweets.
The wonder,
What change a day can bring,
Though so short that moment lived,
For we would later learn of one sad thing,
That a day can take back what happiness it brings.
The bad news was,
We found out that our parents would be leaving.
And tears welled up in my eyes,
While you were screaming,
Making painful noises,
For we were not going home,
And would still have to face,

The days ahead,
In that dreadful place,
The Belize City Hospital,
The staff like guards,
The nurses, their needles,
And that awful ward.

Grevenio!
Lucky for us both,
The visits from our parents became frequent.
Still you hardly spoke,
But I knew what silence meant.
On those days when we waited,
And a parent did not come to visit,
We, the little rascals rendered helpless,
Were left with no will to fight,
While searching for a way out,
Through the long days and nights,
When nurses continued to show up,
With our medication, and
Needle in hand,
The moments repeating themselves,
When we wished escape by sea or land,
Or even by air,
And hoped someone would ring a freedom bell,
To make us strong,
Lest we'd give up,
And at length would die,
Wishing a drink from freedom's cup,
While seeking answers,

Asking Jesus, "Why?"

Grevenio!
Then came another moment,
One which would make my day brighter.
While you slept in silence,
An orderly offered to take me,
Down to the theater.
The nurses changed my gown,
As I acted like the friendliest child.
And half the staff stood around,
Since this dressing and inspection took a while.
And oh, the excitement for me then.
Even the doctor smiled.
And each nurse became my friend,
For I was, after all, a most lucky child,
Unlike the previous days.
Having been taken to the theater before,
As a younger lad living in Belize City,
And had come to love it.
My excitement drew laughter,
And as the nurses cheered me on,
I smiled in my innocence,
Then an orderly pushed me,
Down that long corridor, in a wheelchair,
Towards the operating room.

Grevenio!
Twenty-four hours later, as I recall,

I awoke on my bed,
On a quiet, peaceful day,
Still with a sleepy head.
I found the doctor squeezing my hand,
And he said to me:
"Good, now you're fine, my man!"
But gee!
I wondered what had transpired.
What did they do?
For there was no memory of a picture show,
That I'd seen the day before.
Everything changed, and
I'd been given a new beginning,
But it was all so strange,
The trip to the theater,
And back to my ward,
How rested I felt.
Then the good news came,
I was to go home,
Very soon
My father arrived to take me home,
And there I last observed you, Grevenio, alive,
With a kind of lonesomeness reflecting in your eyes.

Grevenio!
I can still see you on your bed,
And me travelling on the bus,
Trying to clear my aching head,
My eyes full of the flying dust,
While my parents were taking me,

Towards our home in the village.
Often the bus was engulfed by a sea
Of flaring dust from the white maul.
For in those days,
That's what the roads were made of.
I watched them lead in different directions,
To various locations,
And tracked each by the flying dust,
For it was something to do,
When I wasn't thinking
Of you,
There remaining.
And, as time went by
So many years passing,
Decades on the fly,
Still, Grevenio,
You stayed on my mind.

The Chase

M r. Orlando, the farmer, a troubled man,
    The children made him mad,
And choked up with anger,
After fruits,
Fell from his trees,
Shaken by a boy,
Who like a common thief,
Picked up hands full,
Of the mangoes to eat.
Fruits so yellow, so sweet.
And while the farmer slept,
 Boy figured they never would meet.

Yonder on the edge of the old man's farm,
Down by the wire,
Farmer Orlando had pledged,
A strong desire,
To shoot that thief,
Of the forbidden fruits.
Yet the boy was not careful,
Went wherever he would,
First, Chi-Chi birds to shoot.
Then he examined each fruit,

Some ripe, some rotten under lush trees,
He climbed, he chuckled, and he began to reap.

Soon sunset came,
And the sky turned orange.
There was a shower of rain,
That woke up the farmer.
He looked through his window,
Saw something in the head of a tree:
"Hay Dios Mìo! El *boy berry bad*", he shouted,
In a half-Spanish, accented rage.
"él no afraid no, bad boy?
Thief da fruits too much!"
Then in an instant, the chase began,
Fast as lightening; the boy ahead, the farmer behind.

Some villagers watched,
In awe as they went,
Changing directions,
They vanished from sight.
Boy at full speed,
 farmer puffing behind,
Shotgun in hand, and
Shooting away.
But that barefoot, bad boy, wasn't
Hanging around.
And soon, the old farmer,
Was exhausted and done.

The Snake That Chased My Mother

N o sibling of mine had ever seen,
　　Anything as strange as this.
On one sunny day in May,
A snake began to chase our Mother.

Around our house my Mother ran,
As fast as she could go,
Till she decided to stop and stand,
And face that dreadful creature.

Half a dozen children stood with me,
In shock, speechlessly staring.
Till the neighbor, Smith, asked about Gwen,
"What's chasing her?" He was inquiring.

The old man saw a piece of Henequen string,
Tied to my Mother's dress, and he got her attention.
The nine of us burst into laughter,
While mother held her chest, and Smith quipped:
"Oh, what an awful snake!"

Remembering Teakettle Village

The village sat-
Its streets unpaved-
When times were tough-
I came of age.

The farm spread wide-
Its produce was life-
Father grew corn-
I tended rice.

Days were long-
The sun was fire-
Sweat soaked my back-
I couldn't retire.

Evening walks taken-
In cool and color-
I remember the girls-
Each had her fellow.

I was poor-
And dreaming of Heaven-
Girls looked for cash-
The poor was forsaken.

So, alone I lingered-
On village streets-
Except for my siblings-
Few folks were sweet.

But I came of age-
And ran into love-
That Angi was mine-
Were the best of times.

We held hands-
Though the days were hot-
I kissed her lips-
And that was a lot.

But time got short-
When we were together-
She moved on-
And I left forever.

Now decades passed-
Since I left to travel-
Time flew by fast-
Left my feelings unsettled.

Looking back-
I long for the village-
Nothing replaces-
Its streets and its faces.

Sir Victor Albert Lamb
(The New Principal)

The new principal at Saint Francis Primary School,
    Was so unlike the old,
He threw out proper protocol,
We students thought him awfully bold.

One morning, the fearless, principal came,
He stepped right into the Standard Six classroom,
Totally drunk, completely insane,
And laughter broke out soon.

He had on a big, short underpants,
With slippers on his ashy feet.
Straight up before the class he pranced,
And that sucker began to teach.

Not one student paid attention,
And that made the new fellow exceedingly mad.
He whipped each student to great confusion,
And insisted each should tell his or her Dad.

A Moment of Prayer

L ent at school was a season for the church,
  Roman Catholic teachers, priests, and nuns.
They observed Lent for God's love,
I kept it up for fear of the Above.

Eleven then, I was a coward lad,
Not Catholic, Pentecostal, Methodist–nothing.
"A troublemaker!" Fred, my neighbor said,
"That's why you're so afraid of the dark."

I knelt at the feet of the crosses, the stations,
And pretended to pray like a pious Catholic,
But my friend Jun and I swapped jokes during prayer time,
 we couldn't remember the lines.

It all came down to this,
That each night I had to go past,
The haunted S-Curve, said to be the home of a ghost.
Then I tried hard to forget my jokes.

One night I approached the S-Curve,
And there stood my neighbor's dead friend.
In fear I fretted, felt strangely cold, so I said a solemn prayer,
And In less than a minute, I became a devoted Catholic.

The Road to Roaring River

P uddles of muddy water settled on the road,
   Which lead down to Father's corn field.
The rainy seasons soaked it wet,
And we children dug in our heels,
As we skipped along the way,
Passed rapids from the early rains,
Where water flowed swiftly on certain days,
Away from the main,
And down the mountain sides,
Via deep drains,
The yearly deluge made,
Beside the seemingly unending road,
Where we children lagged behind father,
Igniting his wrath,
When he did not understand,
Why so slowly we walked,
And moved along,
Making conversation,
As we hopped from one dry spot to another,
On our way down to that corn field.

At first, there was only a narrow trail,
Half cleared of trees.
For here and there the workers had failed,

To remove a stump.
Had left them in the ground,
'Till more time for clearing came,
And equipment was brought in.
Then the workers made some gains,
And the trail was made wider,
A sure comfort to the farmers' brains.
And a good thing for Father,
Whenever he headed south,
Towards the corn field.
But no doubt,
On his way home, he was glad,
And we children felt well,
To have been on a wide-open road,
And not almost knee deep in mud,
After each shower of rain
Brought another nasty flood.

In time, we children learned,
When to run ahead,
Or walk beside Father,
Or behind him.
Yet,
It was not long before,
We realized that,
Not much had changed.
For the once narrow trail,
Had only been made wider,
And the puddles of muddy water became,
More interspersed,

Especially at the place where Father and
We children entered the road.
Then again where we got off.
And where it continued, on its winding way,
Beyond Father's corn field,
And beyond his watermelon patch,
Where green vines ran every-which-way,
Deep down in the valley.

Often the walk left me tired, but thinking,
Not of the muddy water on the road,
Nor of the many tracks of a jaguar,
Nor of the horses
That some farmers used,
To trek back and forth,
But I wondered,
Where that lonesome road went,
And wondered more,
Each time it was made wider,
And dumped with white maul.
Material the ancient Maya used,
All over the Yucatan Peninsula,
Packed hard into concrete-like slabs,
Solid in the summertime,
But soft and slushy in the rainy seasons.
I kept thinking as I grew older,
When trips to the corn field with my brothers
And with Father,
Became more frequent.

We children followed Father,
Like young ducklings imprint their mother.
We walked ankle deep in the mud.
Deeper in the muddy water.
And even at the onset of dry seasons,
The mess remained for weeks,
Before all the slush was gone.
And each dry season lasted,
March through April, and often into May.
The fifteenth of May!
An old farmer once told me,
"*Man, you see.*
Get your seeds into the ground,
before the fifteenth.
For after that date,
the rains will come pouring down,
with a vengeance."
And the rains came every year,
Unannounced and unimpeded.

I shall always remember, and
Never forget,
Those rainy days.
Though I've had some regret,
When, on certain days, we children
Reached home from the fields,
Our clothing soaking wet,
By multiple showers of rain.
The most precious gifts from the sky,
For then we had rainwater to drink.

And Father,
He said: "Thank God for it all,"
Though often I gave little thanks,
Or had little appreciation for the rains,
After I'd shivered in the cold,
Drenched in the water.
And my heart pumped like a jackhammer,
And my teeth chattered,
While my skin crawled with what we villagers called,
cold seeds.[9]

Even now, over a quarter century later,
As I remember the rains,
I shiver at the memory of it all.
Such sweet coldness, the wetness.
And yet on many days, I used to wish to God,
That Father did not own a cornfield,
And that the rain would go away,
Or better were it not to come at all.
Or that it would only fall on late evenings,
Upon the roof,
Under which I slept each night.
For anyone aware of the tropics,
And subtropical regions of the world,
Would attest to the truth of
How beautiful it is,
When one is falling asleep,
On a dark and
Lonesome night,

---

[9] *Cold seed* means 'goose bumps' in Belize Kriol.

With the sounds of raindrops,
Making music on a roof.

Year after year,
Summer after golden summer,
When the sun stripped the trees bare,
Except for the evergreens,
Across that vast rain forest,
At Society Hall
And further back along the banks of the Roaring River,
We children followed Father,
Down to those fields,
Which grew larger every year,
With additional patches
Of sugar cane,
Sweet potatoes,
Squash of several varieties,
Okra trees with vines of string beans
Choking the life out of them.
And the weeding became overwhelming,
For Father
And for us all,
Down on his farm.

There a lad can run into trouble,
And, yes, I did,
When on occasions,
Trouble showed up in several forms,
Like a huge hornet's nest,
Or other kinds of wasp nests,

Accidentally cut open
By the machete I wielded,
Or trouble in the form of a snake,
A nine-foot-long boa constrictor,
Sliding towards me.
Once I jumped back with my machete,
And Father reached,
For his sixteen-gauge shotgun.
But the boa slid past him and me,
Before I was able to run.
Then Father saw it again,
Moving swiftly,
Choosing a distinctly, different direction,
As Father's shotgun snapped repeatedly.

We kept going to the fields,
And returning to the main,
As summers passed
And rainy seasons came.
They lasted,
Ever longer,
The showers pouring down,
Upon us in the fields,
With a stubborn will,
Perhaps to fill and flood everywhere,
With muddy water,
As if intending to
Drown us all,
Before Father can gather,
A harvest of corn.

Yet, he always did and always said:
"The rain is
a glorious blessing,"
After the long, dry season.
And we live on, and on.

Better days came,
With wonderful harvest times,
When on moonlit nights,
My family joined,
The good, caring neighbors.
And we all gathered,
In our front yard,
A little enclave within the larger pasture,
By the old family house.
 A home father himself built.
We collected old truck tires,
Poured kerosene oil on them
To light the fires,
And the flames flared,
The glares reaching for the sky,
With orange-yellow tongues in the moonlight.
 Everyone gathered around,
The moment to enjoy.
And often, we children fell asleep,
On the grassy ground.

We woke up,
In time for the start of another fire.
This one lit,

With a different kind of fuel.
The sapodilla wood burned,
And broke down,
Into piles of incandescent coals,
That roasted not fast, but slowly
The green-corn we had placed,
One by one in horizontal rows,
As when the corn was planted,
In the fields.
We children added,
Sweet potatoes,
Green plantains,
Okras, and young bananas
Tipped with salt and pepper.
Then we waited,
While the girls played Ring-a-Roses,
And they danced around.

At midnight, we cheered
In the most beautiful, summer weather,
Because the roasted corn was ready,
 Though not the sweet potatoes,
But the plantains were done,
 the okras, and the young bananas.
Then we had a lot, which
Filled each night with fun.
For We farmers had grown
Almost everything we roasted,
Collected them from the farm,
The meat from the wild.

We had game meat, Father
Brought in from the bushes,
In the hottest days,
Of dry season,
Having hunted birds and antelope,
Days and nights,
In hope,
His children would like that.

The years flew by,
'Till I was in my early teens,
Filled with youthful boasts,
And futuristic dreams,
'Till at long last I took a chance,
And pushed by a curious mind,
Advanced,
Further down that road to find,
Where in this wide world it went,
Though I'd by then figured it out.
So, I walked on past some cedar trees,
On past a swamp filled with noisy frogs,
Until I was near a small pine forest,
Dotted with pollack trees flowering,
And as from the Eternal Giver,
An orange orchard in full bearing.
There I stopped, ate some oranges, and pondered,
Should I proceed?
Just then I spotted the river, below the orchard,
And the road seemed at an abrupt end.

In life one oft' goes down many roads,
Some not ever before imagined.
And one's mind may weigh with loads,
Of dreams and curiosity.
Thus, on life's way,
I've since gone down many roads,
Yet none as revealing,
When I breathed a sigh of strange relief.
And since then I've never again wondered,
Where in this wide world it went.
Though I later learned it did go further yet,
Beyond that place where silently I stood,
Beyond the south bank of the Roaring River,
Across from where I'd stood,
The crystal-clear water flowing, and
In the backdrop, the mountains blue with mist.
At last, I'd left my childhood years behind,
Left my father and his cornfields,
Left my sweet mother thinking,
And I was going to travel further on.

Morvin Thomas

A doctor told Morvin Thomas,
He was about to die.
Life was a race he'd run,
To his friends he should say goodbye.
He shook hands with the villagers,
And spoke kindly to all.
His reason was simple,
He'd come to the end of life.

The old man was not proud,
But humble instead.
He never was loud,
And a good life he'd lead.
But now his time on earth was short,
Though he knew not exactly when.
Death he believed, would come from the North,
And suddenly, on him it would descend.

A coffin was constructed,
Morvin Thomas' size,
It was then fitted,
With linen inside.
And the days went by,
As did the weeks and months,

But the old man did not die,
In fact, he lived on by and by.

The coffin was hung high,
Up inside the old man's house.
It stayed there for a very, long time,
Suspended with ropes
From the loft.
It signaled the end of all hopes,
It caught the villagers' eyes,
Hanging above Morvin Thomas's living room.

The children played under the coffin,
That mahogany box of wood well milled.
They ran, they jumped,
As time moved on with a stubborn will.
Some folks predicted,
Morvin Thomas that fight would win,
Despite the fact,
That death was looking for him.

The story goes on,
But I know nothing about the end,
Morvin Thomas is gone,
I was informed by a gossiping friend.
I'd left the village,
A young man back then,
But I remember Morvin Thomas,
A quiet, humble, and honest gentleman.

Beginnings

B ad and rotten", my neighbor says of me,
"and black as night is dark.
Blackest of all his mother's
Thirteen children."
So, I spend my time trying to be good,
And right, and better.
I'd be better than them all,
And from this goal I shall never falter.

So, I the little black lad,
Begin to go to the hill-top church,
To pray to God to take my sins,
But someone breaks a wind,
And this convinced the good pastor,
To throw me out,
For sinners like me should not be there,
But we should reap whatever Hell we sow.

Bad lad, black as night is dark,
I take a few days off from school,
Ride the neighbor's horses,
Break customs, traditions, and rules.
"Good God!" swore the old man born Jamaican,
"I've known many *ha* lads,

But never comes to mind,
Heny as bad."

On days of almost endless fun, a ten-year old,
I am at every party, public and private,
In and out of the village.
I sleep at the houses of friends
Who hide me from my parents, and theirs.
A week away from home,
Would make my family appreciate me more,
And see the good in me they couldn't see before.

The days are long,
The dry season's on.
Now I can roam far away from home,
Far from the village, and into San Ignacio Town.
But a neighbor sees me there,
At the fair,
And to my parents she whispers,
The pretense, she cares.

On early mornings,
Mother makes much fuss to get me out of bed,
She shakes my sleepy head,
Get up I must,
Before the big man calls,
(My Father is not small).
Should I tarry, he shouts,
Then I jump right up and move about.

But never do I fail,
To be ready to go to the farm,
Early in the morning,
After tea is taken,
And hot Johnny Cakes are eaten.
Wide awake,
I run down to the farm,
And sow the seeds of corn.

It takes me an hour to reach the farm,
Plantation we villagers say.
At times, a light drizzle falls and
Foxes run into the bush,
Where trees are tall as structures built by man,
And valleys green are lush with these.
We'd slash and burn before we sow the seeds,
On days as hot as fire.

I sip from the water jug,
A precious moment of taste,
Unless I swallow a bug,
Then the water goes to waste,
While Father watches me,
With eyes red as blood.
I wish for night,
And for the comfort of my bed.

The sun is high overhead,
But work is done today,

My neighbor comes by from his farm,
His daughters following.
They call for me to run along,
On the walk back to the village,
And I do with utmost haste,
Cause I am their friend.

The afternoon finds me at home,
Surprise! Aunt Thay is visiting.
She brings Cousin Harry along,
The lad who laughs hysterically at my jokes,
Before we rob the breadbasket,
Of "Sacred" stuff my Mother bakes,
On every Friday before the sunset signals,
The Sabbath Day is come.

My parents go to church on Saturdays,
And they pray for everyone.
For me–the lad who's bad,
Rotten, and black as night is dark.
For my brothers who can get awfully mad,
During a fight,
And for my sisters who are always glad,
Because they're treated right.

On the evening before Aunt Thay leaves,
There's food for all, a family reunion.
I recite a poem on this dry-weather night;
Applause! Then it is time for bed.
Harry and I talk till night's almost past.

We talk of girls we love,
Discuss their beauty, not their brain,
And Speak of things we'd love to do with them.

The time comes.
Aunt Thay and Harry will leave on the bus,
It'll take them into Belize City,
After good luck wishes,
Hugs, and loving family kisses.
Then I am alone again,
As though I have not seven brothers,
Because my friend, Cousin Harry, is gone.

I turn back to village friends, and we kick football,
Sometimes from noon till night.
Sprain my ankle, twist a toe.
I limp for weeks at a time,
In painful moments while I heal,
And old Man Vasquez rubs my feet,
And washes them with alcohol.
I feel helpless and sad.

But old Man Vasquez is a determined fellow,
And I'm required to see him every day,
So, he can apply the ointment, greasy and yellow,
Until finally he says: "Son, you're OK".
Then I can run again, as before,
And carry on,
And try not to be a bad lad anymore,
As my young life is prolonged.

But again, I run away from home,
Go on hunting trips,
Deep into the Roaring River Valley,
Where I roam through the lush rain forest,
Stopping here and there to fish for bay snooks.
I accompany grown men who pay in cash,
I carry loads of fish and game-meat,
And find in this much pleasure.

At last, I go back to school,
And am present in class,
Must learn and follow each rule,
But I show up not for Catholic Mass,
Because my folks are Pentecostal,
And though I was not,
My parents' words are final,
Whenever I choose to obey them.

Mother looks thoughtfully at me,
Wondering what, I do not know, but
We talk late at night when other siblings sleep,
And she begs me not to skip school again,
But go to church, help the neighbors on their farm,
And carry water from the pump to their homes.
But I fall asleep on the chair,
And I don't wake up until sunrise.

Mi Dandy

Mi Dandy is a businessman, a grocer, a farmer.
He stands six feet tall, but seems taller,
When he walks and wanders on the village.
Little children, teenagers, adults to him call,
As he walks proudly,
On afternoon strolls.
Mi Dandy holds his head high,
He says he lives in a turbulent world,
Full of village fools who file by.
Yet, he waves his hands at them
As they call out to him,
"Mi Dandy, Mi Man!"

Some villagers think that Mi Dandy is a wise man,
Perhaps, the wisest man in Teakettle village,
But he says he is no friend of theirs,
For they're all fools and foes,
Who upon these pathways go.
Yet, he stops here and there to talk with them,
And sincerely shakes his head,
When one inquires how he still walks among the living,
And not among the dead,
After slugs slammed into the wall,
Of his grey, grocery shop, where he faked that fatal fall,

Seconds before the blast of the gunshots.

Mi Dandy walks on and on each day,
He dresses like a soldier duty bound,
In khaki clothing,
He makes his daily rounds,
Up and down the dusty roads,
Colonial hat upon his head,
16-gauge shotgun in his hand,
Ready to shoot off a load,
If by chance he sees Robert, that fool,
The little man who swore to see him slaughtered.
And sometimes, Mi Dandy shoots off a load,
A loud blast to warn his enemies and everyone.

When he is in the shop shifting around,
He waves his hands to passersby,
And his blood-shot eyes look over the counter,
At customers where they stand,
Or lean on the crude counter,
While he tells stories to those,
Who willingly wait their turn to be served.
Mi Dandy closes his eyes and laughs at them.
Some leave laughing, while others linger on,
For not then, or ever, are some in a hurry.
They're there, not to learn,
But to tease.

Some to hear the words of wisdom that Mi Dandy speaks.

He teaches them from day to day,
That young villagers must wisdom seek,
And change their cheating ways.
Children are to go to school,
Learn how to work and run a farm,
Or they'd all become poor fools,
Not unlike their parents.
Thus, Mi Dandy solemnly warns,
Before he laughs, and laughs, until
Tears flow and fall from his bulging eyes,
Then he can barely see.

The farm is first for which Mi Dandy lives,
He sells his produce and everything he grows,
And seldom does Mi Dandy gives.
He says that nothing is free,
Pretends to count the fruits on every tree,
Lest his children and their rascal friends begin to take,
Thinking he runs a charity and mangoes are free,
And they can take till season ends,
When the rains begin to fall,
Upon the driest ground,
And customers no more call,
Or come to stand around.

Mi Dandy's strength declines,
But not his mighty mind.
He tells everyone that he is fine,
While he works harder on the farm,
Because there is no produce left to sell,

To those who still come to buy,
Though some are there to give him hell.
Mi Dandy says they're cheating fools,
And liars like their parents.
They seek wealth, but will never work,
Though Mi Dandy needs workers on his farm,
Men who from work would never shirk.

So, Mi Dandy selects a group of young men,
He says they're rascals he can teach,
Who would become beggars otherwise,
And Mi Dandy gives them a feast,
Before the days of work begin,
At the upper farm that he owns,
And those who don't come to work will commit a crime.
They'd be like dogs that run off with a bone.
Nevertheless, Mi Dandy always gains,
Because he sows, and sows, and sows,
And oh, the huge harvest of grain he reaps,
And the display of produce that he shows.

He sells his produce at the market in Belmopan,
Supplements with fruits he buys and sells,
But for this he hires a special crew,
Promises to pay them well.
Then Mi Dandy takes the men to Rocky Nar,
Down deep in orchards far,
Where oranges are sold,
But at noon the reapers rebel.
They become angry souls,

Because Mi Dandy buys hard-time biscuits for lunch,
Instead of "rice and beans- stewed chicken- and salad",
The favorite Belizean dish.

I stand silently by,
Because the men are weary, angry souls.
Harsh words begin to fly,
From the reapers young and old,
Caused Mi Dandy to cry.
And oh, the crocodile tears that flow and fall
From Mi Dandy's eyes,
Until the men decide to heed his call.
They load the fruits into the bus,
Which takes us all to Belmopan,
Where Mi Dandy apologizes to the men,
And once more gains their trust.

The days of working end,
And Mi Dandy walks the village streets no more.
Still he is visited by the fools,
Who insist on darkening his door.
They discuss the old days on the farm,
The parcels of land that Mi Dandy owns,
And the huge harvests of corn he sold.
He boasts, he'd never begged a bank for a loan.
But retirement leaves Mi Dandy bored,
He longs to hear Marcus Garvey speak again,
As in the days of old,
When Mi Dandy was young and had a good brain.

Life is such that it fades with time,
The clock ticks on from day to day,
And with it, Mi Dandy's health declines.
And no more walks he in his awful ways,
But now he speaks of God's eternal will,
While foolish people visit still,
As they did, even on his wedding day.
Now peacefully Mi dandy rest on cemetery hill,
While his words of wisdom remain.
And village fools must carry on,
If, indeed, the lessons can learn,
They might get past Mi Dandy's scorn.

Nostalgia

I sit here in silence,
On this cold, winter night in Minnesota.
A moment which takes me back in time,
And thrills me with sweet memories of my past.
The old days come back to mind,
And I remember some long-forgotten things,
Which once seemed insignificant,
So long ago, gone.

I remember my childhood ways,
And how simple village life used to be,

My elementary school days,
the huge Hog-Plum Tree.
It stood tall above the Teakettle Creek Bridge,
Stood there for half the years,
It took me to grow up,
Down in Teakettle Village.

My mind surveys my past,
The place where that hog plum stood,
High above the creek,
Near where Miss Lou collected firewood,
Now long gone, may she rest in peace,
Though still I see her standing near that bridge,
Below which I sometimes hid,
On days when I skipped classes.

The memories come with deepest thoughts,
A magical moment lingering.
My past, a vertical chart.
I remember the old school building,
And the truck named Fina-G,
Parked up high upon the hill,
For all the students to see,
That it was there.

At the end of classes on each school-day,
The sounds of voices roared,
As the children made their way,
From the school yard to the top of the hill.
I can almost see the owner of the school truck,

Hear him speak,
Shouting at the rowdy students,
Rushing to climb aboard Fina-G.

My heart aches as I remember the P.W.D.[10] work men,
Removing that Hog-Plum Tree.
And oh, the angry noises of bulldozers,
While my thoughts flow free,
Like floodwaters in that creek,
Where I spent so many days of classes skipped,
The water when it ran,
Flowed swiftly, in a rapid, downward slide.

I see the water flowing,
As fast as that truck driver swore,
On one day when he made a desperate run,
After Fina-G,
Left out of gear, rolled down the hill.
Still, hauled school children between villages,
Roaring Creek, Camalote, and
Sweet Home of mine–Teakettle.

The memories stop then flow again,
Like soft, sweet music in my head.
I think of the Rascal, Orange Reapers,
And that deepens my moment of thought.
I remember Saint Edmond Campion School,
And the Teakettle Creek bridge,
The truck named Fina-G,

---

[10] P.W.D. is an acronym for Public Works Department.

It's owner and his sons.
They stood strong,
Enduring the years Belize yearned for its Independence.
Endured the years it took me to grow up,
Endured hurricane winds, forest fires,
And the termites' destructive ways.
Tonight, I long for the ancient village days,
For people, places, and things.
Tonight, I'm overcome with Nostalgia.

BOOK TWO
REFLECTIONS ON NATURE

POEMS

A Minnesota Spring Day

M orning and the sunrise is beaming,
   High above the trees,
The lilacs blooming,
Awakened from the freeze.

It's early spring,
The season emerging.
Blades of grass are green,
Fresh from a soaking.

Rain is falling yet again,
As it does each day,
I'm here at work,
Not for spring pleasures, but for the pay.

Only yesterday it was bitterly cold,
Now the sun rises high and bold,
I see it through the window.
A Minnesota spring day, full of surprises.

A Minnesota Summer

A Minnesota summer,
Is a season I treasure,
But like each newcomer
I live it with measure.

A Minnesota summer,
Could fool a newcomer
The lakes and the trees,
Hold a beauty that makes the heart pleased.

A Minnesota summer,
Like spring and fall, is a wonder,
But Minnesota also has a different take,
And I refer not to ten thousand lakes.

I speak now, not as a newcomer,
But as one who was deceived by the weather.
I've learned that a Minnesota summer,
Ain't nothing like a Minnesota winter.

F. Daniel Brackett

A Minnesota Evening

E vening! The day moves on,
And the wind is blowing,
A cold moisture through the air
Where I stand,
Breathing in the change.

Night is almost here,
And if the wind blows colder,
I shall hardly be able to bear,
Inhaling
The cold evening air.

Worry enters my mind,
Because I know-
It's nearing wintertime.
I count the hours as they come and go,
From one cold day to another.

On this evening before winter arrives,
I feel her heavy in the air.
I imagine the snow drifts,
Hear ice popping on the lakes,
And on the Mississippi River.

Winter will soon cloak me,
No good feeling, tidings bear.
While I stand here waiting, inhaling,
The wind never stops,
The cold air blowing.

On Life

It is the rain that gives us water,
The sun that takes it back,
The life we live on earth,
Reveals what we humans lack.

The drops of goodness fall,
In cleansing moments of rain,
Yet some people never stop,
Finding reasons to complain.

When the rain falls,
We cry out for sunshine,
Somehow in this,
We find the peace of mind.

It is the rain that gives,
The sun that takes,
The life we live,
Each of them makes.

The Right Reasons

Like leaves upon a walnut tree,
Are people on earth's shore,
Each allotted a moment to be,
Till that moment is no more.

Leaves once alive in the wind,
With the strength of Nature's will,
They open at the start of spring,
They close with the winter's chill.

Our lives are touched by flowers,
Blossoms cover the trees,
One day this life is ours,
In the next, it's gone with the breeze.

So, let's live for the right reasons,
For Peace and Goodwill here,
As today may bring good seasons,
But tomorrow may not be fair.

One Final Day of Fall

This day of fall brings a sun,
　So bright and beautiful,
I wonder if the Northern Lights
Will paint the evening sky.
Normally, it would be dark,
When I take my evening walk,
Among the trees,
As now I do today.

But this fall day is like no other to me,
It takes away my breath,
As future things I seem to see,
Along life's unstable way.
The weather is getting cooler,
The wind blows stiff and wild,
I am feeling ever colder,
And longing for another season mild.

I'll drive along the North Shore,
Of Lake Superior,
Far away to the north,
Hear the waves crashing on the rocks,
Before the winter freeze.
Then I might see a ship go by,

And feel a gentle breeze,
There among the evergreen.

Just a few days from today,
Everything, everywhere will be white,
And snowflakes will play,
In the cold winter nights.
Then this fall day will be forgotten,
As will this bright and beautiful sun,
The Northern Lights,
And this colorful evening sky.

As I take this walk
Among these trees,
I sense the last of Fall,
I take time to ponder,
And I remember that,
Nothing lasts forever.
Not even this day of Fall,
For soon an angry winter, will engulf us all.

I'm not ready for the cold,
Nor for the wild wind blowing, no,
I turn now to home, to rest my feet.
Tomorrow I'll walk again, if the weather is mild.
I shall walk among the trees,
Hear their leaves play in the wind,
And perhaps enjoy one final day of Fall,
Before the next winter begins.

Whipped

There's a lonesome feeling,
That strikes through my heart,
When winter's coming,
And the snowfall starts.

I sit by my window,
See the snowflakes fall,
I watch winter's shadows,
They cover summer's hall.

I'm cold and fearful,
Unlike life on the tropical farm,
My coat is woolen,
But I'm still not warm.

Lonesomeness I can bear,
Through the thick and thin,
But the cold and the fear,
They beat me from within.

Rainstorm

I watch the rain come tumbling down,
Heavily from the sky.
Yet, the sun keeps shining,
While water storms the ground.

The storm does not slacken,
The sun refuses to fade,
I see a rainbow in the sky,
Above the forest glade.

Colors paint the sky above me,
Red, orange, yellow, green,
I watch the sun at last goes down,
I see a rushing stream.

Dandelions

Dandelions! Dandelions!
  Yellow and white,
The grass can't grow,
You squeeze them tight.

Grass is green,
But you are not,
Yellow and white, with green,
Don't make a match.

Dandelions! Dandelions!
Beautiful and bright,
I'll cut you down,
Tomorrow at daylight.

Smart Storms

S mart storms come and go with spring,
They blow, they gust, they squall,
They splinter trees and houses,
Before they whirl away.

Smart storms come and go with spring,
They blow, they gust at night,
They blacken the sky at day,
Before they whirl away.

Smart storms have brilliant minds,
They choose where next to strike,
Sometimes, they wreck a city,
Sometimes, the farmers' plight.

Sometimes, they fool a weatherman,
They make him blush with shame.
Sometimes, they simply fade away,
And never come back again.

Reflection on Spring

On days when rain would fall,
　　When robins sing and blue jays call,
When the grass grows tall,
I know the season is spring.

When snow has slowly melted,
And the ground is soft and wet,
And tulips dare to sprout,
I know the season is spring.

When days are warm,
And for Summer, the birds call,
I know that winter is gone,
And I know the season is spring.

The Birds

T he birds,
 They fly, they sing, they play,
They have no words to say
Along life's way.

Like the birds, I speak not a word,
I simply watch them play,
Each day I listen to the birds,
I hear them sing along life's weary way.

The birds,
They fly, they sing, they play,
They speak not a word,
They joyously sing each day.

I Do Not Like the Cold

I do not like the cold!
The snow I never mind.
On any wintry day, my life is fine,
Should warmth enclose my soul.

The flakes are falling swiftly,
I watch the snow drifts build,
I Like to see this white world glow,
In the heart of wintertime.

Snowflakes falling softly,
Dressed in white, lace, and frills,
But the cold is here to test my will,
And makes me suffer ills.

Someday, I'll look back at these wintry nights,
Maybe when I'm old,
Some beautiful moment I'll recollect,
But I do not like the cold.

Though I will have survived each winter,
I think I'll never say,
That I was ever happy,
On any cold, winter day.

Down Deep

Down in the oceans blue,
   The fishes live out their lives,
Down below the raging waves,
The fishes swim and dive.

Down within the oceans blue,
The splendid corals grow,
And playful fishes hide,
Where colorful corals glow.

Down upon the oceans' floor,
Down below the tides,
No storm can find the playful fish,
Among the corals where they hide.

Rain Is Falling

Rain is falling on the roof,
And spilling over the ledge,
Where gutters are leak proof,
And fastened on the edge.

Rain drops dive from scary heights,
They holler as they hit the ground,
And still others make their flights,
After water flows around.

People sit and stare at the rain,
At water splashing on the house,
Raindrops help to cool the brain,
When life is at its worst.

The sun rays are all gone away,
But rain keeps coming down,
And so, the air is cool today,
Because raindrops are falling on the ground.

Sunlight

S aturday, and the sun, instead of light,
  Gives off dreariness, like a dream,
While my senses fight,
To find the usual beam.

Sunlight is the life of man,
Photosynthesis the life of trees,
Except for sun we cannot stand,
Or face old winter's freeze.

The morning sits bereft of light,
Dreariness takes over my world,
Yet the day might still get bright,
And help me to fight, what trouble nature hurls.

Nature's Gift

The sun beams through the leafless trees,
Shows its brilliant light,
Shines upon the fallen leaves,
The sun is golden and bright.

Branches reflect sunrays,
Repel the golden sun,
And this in winter days,
Keeps snow upon the ground.

The sun is bright and beautiful,
Beaming through the trees,
This is a wonderful, wintry scene,
Nature's gift to you and to me.

F. Daniel Brackett

Sunset Scenes

S unset scenes above a stream,
 I watch the clouds' colors change,
O'er mountain peaks,
In a sunlit summit range.

In stillness stands this silent range,
Golden below the sky,
Along comes clouds with shadows dark,
And bid the sun goodbye.

Farewells are not forever,
This stream is still unchanged,
In silence sunsets fade away,
Beyond the mountain range.

Thunder Roll

S ounds explode within the clouds,
   Low, noisy thunders rolling by,
Folks look up from the earth below,
What mystery lies up in the sky?

I hear a thunder roll and explode.
Within the clouds, like loud bells toll,
Sky meets Earth at a line of light,
A star is born this very night.

There's something there in space and time,
The atmosphere with clouds combined,
Mysteries meet with power and might,
When thunders roll in the dark, dark night.

The Wind

I hear the wind blowing outside,
   I look to see it go,
I find a fact that nature hides,
The wind I cannot know.

It blows right through my window,
Sounds like an arrow released from a bow,
It crushes a vase, but I cannot see the wind,
It leaves through an open door.

I look out my window,
I say: "There she goes,"
O'er the fields and meadows,
Oh, how the wild wind blows.

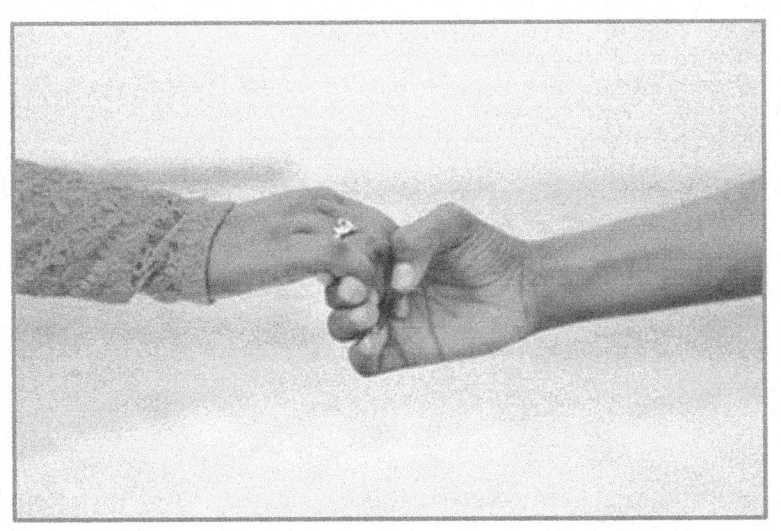

BOOK THREE

LOVE AND FRIENDSHIP

POEMS

I Meet My Friend

For you I find too little time,
    Because the clock is ticking.
How fast the hours pass,
When life would find us meeting.

We talk of successes, trying times and failures,
We feel deep silence in our heart.
Occasionally we smile, we laugh,
Then we reflect upon some art.

Our meeting's like a game of baseball,
Each time we talk is as if we're batting.
The times we bat are like we're asking,
Do we live on or does life passes?

The moment's filled with something majestic,
One throws a ball, the other's batting.
Magic fills the air around us,
A sense of love protrudes.

Our finest times are full of thoughts,
An inner silence while we're talking.
Each moment brings another subject,
But always, the clock is ticking.

A Drifter In Oregon

I drifted into Oakridge,
With the setting sun.
I watched the highest mountains,
That guard the little town.

The days were filled with pleasure,
The nights with light, cool rain.
I dreamed a thousand rainbows,
Sleeping near the 'Main'.

I met a girl named Tina,
Her eyes were soft and blue.
She had a love for nature,
Said she'd hug trees too.

Tina had written poems,
I read some in a day.
I liked the one called "Drift Along",
It stole my heart away.

As I had drifted into Oakridge,
So came my time to leave.
I bid farewell to Tina,
With the setting sun.

Down Memory's Lane

Today I took a walk,
  Down Memory Lane,
Picked flowers in a park,
And got all wet with rain.

Down that lonesome lane,
I walked while thinking back.
I remembered the time when I was young,
And thought I'd fallen in love.

I was young and proud and black,
There was this sweet, Latina Girl.
Her padre begged her to move on, not to look back,
But I was caught up in her Latin world.

Too late it was for her father,
Since we'd already kissed.
Sweet child, her daddy's daughter,
Was already living in my world.

Though love seemed strong,
We soon moved apart.
But now I ask myself repeatedly,
Was that really love?
Hallelujah! It certainly was.

P. J.

Down in Georgia where peaches grow,
I met a girl who was white as snow.
She stole my heart with a Georgia smile,
So, I stayed in her town for a little while.

Down in Georgia where peaches bloom,
That girl kept my heart one afternoon.
The sweetest little girl I'd ever seen,
She said that her name was Pamele Jean.

Down in Georgia, the peaches state,
I had to decide what would be my fate.
I fell in love with that Georgia sky,
But Pamele Jean was the reason why.

Oh, the land of peaches
And pies!
Down in Georgia,
Where I said good-bye.

Courtship

A summer sweet,
When love was young,
That we would meet,
Each other found.

'Twas like a dream,
When we got together.
A Canadian scene,
Mountains and evergreens.

She sat by the lake,
I took her picture.
Sweet, White date,
And a Black suitor.

To A Friend From A Friend

Y our throne is high,
　　Oh, Queen of Conquest.
You sit on your throne,
And your judgement is harshest.
Scepter in hand,
I cannot stand.

Like a judge you read the charges.
Your judgement looms in front of me,
No mercy I could see.
Someday repealed,
The wrongs you feel,
Will prove my innocence.

I am that friend put upon.
No words can flow,
I feel that blow.
Your pride was broken down.
Words cannot tell,
But your judgement is hell.

A Wife

A wife is like an anchor,
  She holds the ship called Man,
When upon an ocean tossed,
The anchor keeps him safe and sound.

No ship sails upon the seas,
Without an anchor on its deck.
No man lives a fulfilled life,
Without his darling wife.

Sail not now, nor ever,
Upon the sea of life,
Unless you have your anchor,
The help that is your wife.

Each time a ship sets sail,
It's like when a man is borne.
Like a ship, he drifts for a while,
But soon for a wife he yearns.

Enough

I t is in deep thought that I engage,
Myself in conversations.
I talk myself out of my rage,
By verbal contemplations.

This dilemma oft' occurs,
My wife hears me call her name.
I did not, though I concur,
I spoke only to myself; it's not the same.

I wonder if she listens,
Thinking I'm losing my own head,
Sometimes, I mumble nothing,
But she hears her name instead.

Moments To Live For

Weekend mornings are
      Moments to live for,
And when I am awakened,
I'm given to a lore.

It's the thought of an early breakfast,
Or a simple cup of tea,
With eggs fried quickly,
Scrambled, or over-easy.

But it annoys me that,
My wife keeps interrupting,
Perhaps, to ask for the keys,
Or to discuss something uninteresting.

Then as the time files by,
My morning just grows dim.
Breakfast gets awfully cold,
Even the birds don't bother to sing.

Yet for these moments I live,
Weekends do make my life.
What must I do or give,
To keep them peaceful and bright?

Daughter

L ove is tender and kind,"
　　Someone wrote,
And in this line, I find,
The blessings he spoke.

Blessings like you, my Little Flower,
With innocence in your eyes,
Holds my heart forever,
You're my own special prize.

You are my champion,
Young as early spring.
My heart's companion,
For you I sing.

Oh, Daughter of Love,
Gift of nature,
And of God above.
Nothing in life matters like Love.

Love is tender and kind,
And ever present in your father.
This in the world you'll find,
As you explore further and further.

To Robin
(My Confession)

R obin, you might forgive me, Girl,
     While I try to forgive myself.
Despite your love for me,
And mine for you,
That love I did not affirm.
But you were brave to say,
You loved me
Dearly,
And deeply,
And with a passion
I clearly felt,
But did not embrace.

The truth of my life was what I feared,
And my love was kept concealed,
Throughout that decade in Belize,
While we laughed and talked,
And joked together,
In those dry seasons.
And on evenings when,
The sunlight blazed
On your rich, brown skin,
And the wind sifted,

Through your hair,
Down in Ladyville Village.

You were so beautiful,
To these eyes of mine!
And you still are,
And you'll always be,
The one true fountain of joys,
Of love I never explored,
Despite my pretended rejection of you,
The cruelty of the pain I inflicted,
Upon myself, and you, by sheer denial,
The decades of unspoken dreams that followed,
The times when our eyes met
In the most intimate glances.

Now here in these lines I make,
Not an awkward apology,
But my deepest confession,
Admission.
Indeed, my acknowledgment.
You were right,
And I was wrong.
Of this I am certain—
From the first time our eyes met,
I fell in love with you.
And my love for you grew,
Each time we met thereafter.

Love burned and blazed in my heart.

For how long, I cannot say,
For I have not,
Looked upon you,
Or met you in decades.
And all I have left are,
The memories of those early years.
The times when we were together,
When minutes passed like hours,
While waiting on the bus.
We'd pretend to be just friends,
But we fooled no one.

Today I sit here in my office,
Eyes forward, mind adrift.
I look out the window,
Which opens upon a lake,
And I ponder the past,
My loss.
The sweetness of those moments,
The minutes, the hours,
The days, the weeks,
The months,
The wonderful years
That could have been.

On this cold Minnesota day, I'm dreaming.
My thoughts move back across the distance
Of time,
Of miles, towards our Belize.
O'er the Gulf of Mexico, the Yucatan Peninsula.

They move across that vast rain forest,
Dotted with ancient Maya ruins.
I see you now, as beautiful as you were then,
And you can still see me.
Our eyes meet; I feel the love!
We're together again,
And I am forgiven.

Missionary Girl
(In Memory of My Friend Elva)

M issionary Girl, who made you cry?
Your tears fell fast,
Flowing from your eyes.
Each time was to be the last,
Yet again you cried,
And again, tears fell from your eyes,
But I had no shame,
And I feared not Hell.

I played the board-game with you,
My partner against your sister and her friend.
We lost every time, the games not a few.
Yet, you partnered with me until the end,
And the crying went on for many years.
I joked and I teased,
I played on your fears,

'Till time alone would make me cease.

The years flew by seasons wet or dry,
The board-games stopped,
I don't know why.
But we grew up,
And I saw you not
For a long, long time.
Then we met again, and you were fine.
And I knew that day, there would be no crying.

We played one final game together,
Against your sister and her friend.
You partnered with me,
And we were the best of friends,
The little, white child,
And the skinny, black lad.
Missionary girl, I made you cry,
Then I made you laugh again and again.

Friend
(For Adria, For All the Laughter We Shared)

Y ou're like a flower young,
    Unfolding in the morning light,
You bloom in the evening sun,
And sleep throughout the silent nights.

Not stifled by the scars of life,
Your dreams are bigger than the day,
And like the young flower bright,
You've found a fulfilling way.

Now here you are at a new beginning,
This is an early start.
You're so beautiful, and bright!
You'll find great joy unending.

Love Lost and Found

L ove passed me by,
   She travelled on her way,
A saddened soul,
My life grew cold,
She'd left me mute that day.

Love was then gone,
She travelled far away,
She gave no thought to me.
I'd hoped in vain,
But I moved on.

The years flew by,
Like empty scenes,
Love left me there,
With naught but dreams.
Yet life went on and on.

Time can seem short,
In moments long,
Years passed are naught,
Love can't be bought,
For me she held surprises.

One moment in time,
Feelings flew high,
Love did not pass me again.
She'd stopped and called my name.
I held her close to me.

Her breasts were sweet,
Her lips alluring.
Love held me fast,
Forget years past.
The moment seemed unending.

I Think Of You
(For Lu With Love)

I think of you,
When the day is young,
I think of you,
In the morning sun.

I think of you,
When the day is gone,
When the sun goes down,
And I sing my song.

I think of you,
When I dream at night,

As the stars come out,
And the moon gives light.

My thoughts,
Deep in my heart,
They're not a few,
When I think of you.

Estrella

Estrella! Estrella!
The light of the night.
Estrella! Estrella!
Makes all things bright.
You were a star in my dream,
The night that we met,
The beautiful girl,
I had to forget.

The way your eyes set,
In the darkest night,
Even the city lights fade.
Just for a moment,
You were the brightest light.
But Estrella! Estrella!
There's a dark side to your world,
And that I had to escape.

My Dream

L ast night I penned a short note–
To someone special–from my heart.
I told her of my love and wrote,
In perfect Grammar and in art.

As I remember, this I wrote,
About how much I love that girl,
And how it started with a joke,
A silly joke, yet one that spoke.

This girl I love is exquisite,
Lovely, intelligent, special, and unique.
Unlike many, unlike few,
I love Lu.

Sometimes I love too deeply, in such a simple way,
And I fear she might not be in love with me.
Yet fear will fade away,
And love will shine its brightest light today.

I folded my short note last night,
Before the rushing wind awoke me,
and the morning sunlight came through.
Then I was alone. No note! just the beautiful light,
From my sweet dreams last night.

Shevada

You're a dream so true,
   Oh Shevada,
Like one enduring tune.
It remains after,
Music is played,
And it lingers on.

I think of you, Dear,
With a passion.
Your still penetrating stare,
Is my fashion.
For me, your music remains,
Sustained.

You're like a dream in truth,
So distant you are,
You appear to be,
Like the evening star,
My Dear Shevada.

Amy

Amy was a girl,
I used to know,
We talked and we laughed,
We ate on the go.

We were friends for a time,
'Till the dark wind blew,
She went her way,
I went mine too.

But sometimes at night,
I dream of that girl,
The beauty, the light,
The mysterious world.

This girl named Amy,
Was sweet from the start,
And when she left,
She'd broken my heart.

My Friends

Some friends are my antagonists,
They bring me confrontations,
Unlike my wife,
And our daily contemplations.

My friends aren't really foes,
They just disagree with me.
Unlike my wife who holds great Faith,
In everything I plan to be.

Some friends share love among themselves,
As strong as hate twixt foes.
But often it's easy to see,
The ploys they play on me.

I know the ugly truth of blunder,
The thought a rival's more a friend,
Or that some friends are scatterbrained,
And I the subject of their game.

So down life's road I walk,
I live with confrontations.
But thanks to my wife, I love my life,
And our daily contemplations.

Over Coffee

R ose so sweetly beholds me,
.... Her eyes regarding.
And I sense the aura, taste my coffee,
Feel the moment lingering.

There's innocence in her eyes,
At times, she speaks no word,
But seems rather sad.
She stares up at the ceiling.

I wrap my thoughts around her,
Wondering what truth, the aura speaks.
What troubles she has seen,
Why this sadness in her eyes?

The heart never laments for naught.
The pain paints pictures on her face.
Images of battles fought,
Of hidden troubles in her heart.

Ours is a love of friendship.
A deep, pure dearness,
Like kinship.
At times, a brief dispute, but friendship.

We seldom meet,
But often call to talk,
Conversations filled with affection,
While the moments pass.

There're gentle hugs, no kisses,
Just what actions friendship allows.
An awesome moment passes,
Time well spent in friendship.

She beholds me again,
Her eyes regarding.
I wonder why the sadness in her eyes,
What troubles lingering?

What Is Love

L ove's a phenomenon I cannot define.
I think sometimes that love is unkind,
When like the waves of an ocean,
It washes the shore of my heart.

Love's like thunders rolling,
Loud, noisy, and free.
Emotions erupting,
Love cannot be defined by me.

Like an avalanche in the heart,
Love slides down deep,
Like snow drifts that rise,
When strong winds meet.

I never can tell when Love is real.
Is it what's in the mind,
Or what the heart feels,
Or is love never defined?

A Celebration Of Your Beauty
(For Tami)

When darkness was overtaken by light,
You in deep silence were born.
The sun made your eyes so bright,
And your smiles all warm.

Like the sun you shine ever,
In the orbits you choose,
A life given to purpose, yet pleasure,
In each lingering moment and hour.

Time will not change the joys you explore,
Places cannot alter your dreams.
Till the sun and the moon fold,
You'll be that beautiful queen.

Cathy's Birthday Celebration

I think I'll eat,
One slice of cake.
It is Cathy's birthday,
And I celebrate.

I don't know how old,
She claims to be.
But I'll be bold,
And guess twenty-three.

Her age does not matter,
Just that the day is grand.
I give my compliments,
To her where she stands.

She's all loveliness,
With smiles of glee.
Cathy's the best,
And the cake is free.

I'll have another slice,
Since I'm eating to a dear friend.
A slice twice, in celebration!
No one will worry, least they offend.

Celestia Lozano

C elestia!
　　You're the personification,
Of an African song,
Set to the tune of a major strain.

You're the beat,
Of many thousands African drums.
Rings on your feet,
Sweet rhythmic sounds upon your tongue.

You're the Golden Girl,
Epitome of all that's bright.
Your laughter is,
The music of my heart's delight.

You're the glow of the light,
That shines within a heart.
Oh, Celestia,
You sound the drums of art.

You are of African blood.
You're the symbol of Love.

One Common Friend

Your Friendship failed,
   One simple test.
It couldn't survive,
When it was tried.
Something evoked your foolish pride,
You crushed Friendship to death.

Your words were harsh,
Your heart lost care,
Our Friendship meant nothing to you.
Still, your life won't end.
It will go on,
Just without one common friend.

Farewell I say to yesterday,
When just being friends,
Was our simple way.
I hope you find,
Should the world be unkind,
I was more than one common friend.

One Special Friend
(For Karen)

F riend of mine,
  You're of one kind.
Your love shines through,
And all my world is you.

Your beauty blossoms,
When your hair flies wild,
And you begin to smile.
It is so awesome.

Oh, gorgeous girl,
In your own world,
There's naught but Joy.
Your limit is the sky.

Commitment

D on and Joyce!
   Full thirty years you gave,
To each other.
Your commitment endures.

You believe in giving,
And you pledged your Love for life.
Ever caring,
Ever sharing.

Jamaican born,
You're proud of your heritage,
And the days spent on the island.
Now here you are in the USA.

How many marriages broken?
How many spouses forsaken?
Yet, here we are celebrating,
Thirty years of a marriage enduring.

Don and Joyce, you held to a pace,
You ran together as in a race,
To live, to give, to show,
That Love can keep growing, more and more.

Many moons have passed,
All lit in different patterns.
When came fusses, fights,
Love guided you through to brighter lights.

Don, one story is told that Joyce
Often tells you how to drive.
Well, to me it's no great surprise,
I've been along, rolling my eyes.

Thirty years you gave,
Sweet Love to each other.
Your commitment endures,
And your love grows ever stronger.

Teenage Love

She was young and shy,
And I, first saw her at the church.
Her eyes, her smiles, Her ambulation.
She looked perfect to me.

We met,
We fell in love.
I with her and she with me,
And maybe, with blessings from God above.

I admired her bright eyes.
She gazed at my deep,
Dimpled cheek,
In silent admiration.

We reasoned we should marry,
Or the love would die.
It would not endure,
And we'd both be sorry.

Years passed in separation,
Still, I shan't forget
Her eyes, her smiles, Her ambulation.
She looked perfect to me.

California Memories

My memories remain of California,
Its dampened nights,
When fog settled down,
On wide open farms.

Roads crisscrossed the valley,
There, land was ripped and made ready
For farmers,
Before they sowed the seeds.

California's Central Valley,
 the San Joaquin,
Bountiful in the Summer,
Year after year.

When fall replaced summer,
The weather was perfect.
In town, Chicanos lingered,
And sweet, Latina girls walked together.

I carried the memories back to Belize,
But left my Heart behind,
In the Central Valley,
Where I'd spent some youthful times.

California days, the memories,
They often come back to mind,
Throughout the years since,
I'd left that valley behind.

My Mexican Brother

I have a brother,
He is from Mexico;
As friends, we couldn't fit,
He let the friendship go.

The guy was cool,
When first we met;
But we argued like fools,
And got all upset.

Sometime later,
We settled this fight;
Now he's my Brother,
And all things between us are right.

Where Leads Your Path

R aymond! Your fight spans,
Ten thousand nautical miles.
You took it into distant lands,
Through rays of burning suns.

Your *cause* is one of troubles,
Of dangers lurking near,
Your desire to help the poor,
That plan stands unfailingly fair.

Is your *cause* on behalf of all society?
For whom do you really fight?
Is it for your political party?
Or is it for your own selfish rights?

May God be with you at achievement,
Help you share the gains equally.
And may you still have an honest friend,
When your goal is accomplished totally.

A Hard Nut To Crack

My white girlfriend smiles,
   Then she laughs out loud,
And begins to think,
Before she speaks another word.
She bursts into laughter,
While I wonder why,
But I figure out,
She has a great sense of humor.

Laughter comes again.
She speaks thereafter,
"You're", says she,
"a hard nut to crack."
Maybe I am indeed.
Why wouldn't I marry her?
If not for her great sense of humor,
Why not for her musical abilities?

She can play the piano,
And can sing as good as any singer I know.
She is beautiful and smart,
Has a good job at the university,
And we both like to travel.
Would do a little more,

Before we settle down,
Maybe right here in Canada.

But all summer long,
She repeats the same refrain:
"You're", she says,
"a hard nut to crack."
And she tries so hard to work,
On the brain of this hard nut.
Maybe, she can crack it,
Perhaps, even break it.

The days pass on,
Her family I must meet.
A bigger nut.
One much harder than me to crack.
But we cruise on down,
To a small Manitoba town,
In a little car, speeding along.
We should not be late.

And oh, the fun and the laughter,
On this long road trip.
But we arrive,
And the humor goes dead,
Because the family's in a state of shock.
Surprise to find out one overlooked fact.
Their future son-in-law,
He is not white, but black.

Now my girlfriend laughs no more,
And her humor evaporates.
Her face is this red rock, because,
Her father's the hardest nut to crack.
But time passes us in conversation.
And one sister asks us to be like the animals,
They never mix one kind with another,
No, never.

Folks flock to the family home,
Even the old grandmother comes to see,
For she wants to meet me,
The big, black buck from Belize.
And everyone has their questions,
And everyone tries to be nice,
And would be nicer yet,
If only I was not black, but white.

We stay for eight hours or more,
Exactly how long, I can't remember.
And oh, the faking of fun for some,
While others act as if they don't care.
But I think that they do,
More than they could bear.
And my girlfriend,
She keeps wiping away her tears.

Someone tells a joke,
Just a few funny lines.
It is quite a reunion,

Everyone laughs.
Then another joke is given,
One funnier than the first,
And this goes on until,
The ice is almost broken.

The matriarch serves dinner,
And I ask my girlfriend's father,
"Sir, please pass the chicken,
The potatoes, and the gravy too.
And can you please pour my coffee,
Before we relax in the living room,
To laugh and talk a little more,
A chance to get better acquainted."

The day ends,
It's time to leave Manitoba,
Where prairies stretch out wide.
From the little farming town,
I bid farewell to the family,
And decided then,
There's no chance I'd ever marry,
Into this nice, little, white family.

My Kenyan Friend

Where are you now, my Kenyan Friend?
　　So many years have passed,
What places have time allowed,
What joys and tears,
Since I left you there in Houston?
What in life has brought you fun?
I wonder, did you walk,
Or did you run away from Texas,
To fight your greatest fear,
And reach your highest mark.
After classes were done,
And the counting began,
To take you into places far away.
To England, perhaps,
In search of your love?
Or was it back to Kenya and your Africa,
Where the lions roar,
And where you can prosper,
And find good fortunes?
An accounting major,
Might find success there.
After Texas and the university,
And all the good times we shared,
Before life lead me away,

And I left in haste that day,
In search of greener pastures.
I carried away Texas in my heart,
And left a part of me behind.

My search took me deep into California,
Its central valley,
Where everything planted grows.
A sign of prosperity for me,
In a different way
Than Texas was.
But Henry,
Who could've known,
Imagined,
Guessed,
Predicted,
That I'd have left so suddenly?
Left Houston without warning,
Without saying good-bye,
And not knowing your last name,
When my mind reflected,
As I boarded the bus,
In the noises of that busy city,
Bustling with people.
I thought mostly of the heat,
The sun bearing down on us all,
And being in a hurry,
With miles to burn,
And the memory of the old man,
Standing there shouting,

And the place behind the shop,
Where Church's Fried Chicken was sold
To folks like you and me.

I can't get these things off my mind.
Would never forget,
So many good times in conversation,
Discussions on love and life and death,
The occasional laughter,
On that evening when you cooked,
That Kenyan dish.
We stayed up late talking,
Before you hit the books,
And I went on home,
Then headed out of town to seek my fortune,
Late -on the following afternoon.
There was no time to go down,
To say good-bye
Before the bus would depart,
And cut through town,
Winding on its way through narrow streets,
Beginning the long journey towards Los Angeles.
Then somewhere down the road,
I fell asleep that day,
And woke up to find,
That I'd long ago left Texas,
Bound for California.
Left Houston and all my friends behind,
Without saying goodbye,
Because I was out of time.

But now there's time, and I can reflect and ask,
Where are you now, my Kenyan Friend?

The Old Mercedes Benz

I was thinking the other day,
   What ever happened to the Mercedes Benz?
How it just disappeared,
At the time that Arnold left.

Many times, we rode in that car,
The miles . . . who would ever know?
And now the memory of the 'drives' lives on,
With thoughts of my friend Arnold.

Dark-brown and huge, that Benz rode like a cruiser,
Knowing exactly where Arnold wanted to go,
Down some street or corner, to hit the freeway,
As we went back and forth to Cottage Grove.

Though now I think mainly of that Mercedes Benz,
I seem, somehow, to remember,
Back in '79,
Arnold also had a nice riding Toronado.

A Cry For Home

Like a sparrow far from its nest,
A longing for home is on my chest,
In this land away from heart,
Towards my home my thoughts depart.

When morning comes, I drift away,
The sunset does not end my day,
For sadness lingers on my mind,
That distant home I cannot find.

I think that life is almost end,
And now I need each childhood friend.
In places where I lived this life,
I seek old comforts tonight.

BOOK FOUR

BEYOND BELIZE

POEMS

F. Daniel Brackett

Journeying

I 've seen the Twin Towers and the New York sky,
They loomed above flood lights.
I've watched a Texan child,
Staring at a distant kite.

I've felt the chill of winter,
It is life up in the North.
I have lived in Minnesota,
And think this is not smart.

My journeys are not over,
True living has just begun.
I still think of the Andean Mountains,
I want to see the Serengeti run.

Spanish Talk

C olorful cultures blended,
   They mingled together,
Down in Cancun, Mexico.
There's the perfect picture.

People went everywhere,
Some simply looking,
Some women blushing at this stranger.
Things became interesting.

Their skin was dark,
Smooth like olives on a tree,
Their eyes carried a spark,
They were so beautiful to me.

Their poise, their walk,
Their lips in talk,
I thought their love would be genuine,
And that made me feel fine.

I was overwhelmed by the spell,
As feelings flooded my heart,
But life was not well,
I could not their language talk.

My Boston Moment
(For Mark)

S pring time near Boston Harbor,
  I love this city,
The smell of freshly cut grass,
The girls so sweet, so lovely.

A haven is here,
As if it comes sliding from the sea,
And the hand of an Angel named Lori,
Reaches out and gently touches me.

Her eyes are like twinkling stars,
Like shining harbor lights
On this spring night,
So elegantly bright.

Boston's a city for lovers,
So vast, so comforting to me,
I touch, I taste, I see.
Boston brings true love to me.

I'm at home here in this city,
It's full of life, of history,
Pleasing to my mind,

Here Love my heart now find.

And so, perhaps, for life, I've already found
Everything I need right here in Boston:
Companionship, the friendship, the love,
The moon, the stars, and the golden sun.

I love this city,
The smell of spring, the scenery, the girls so pretty,
Maybe the best thing I've ever done,
Was to make this trip to Boston.

A Wedding

Two got married,
In a ceremony,
One would never forget.
In a little town,
In a New England State,
Where they found love,
And set the date.
A man can give,
Or simply take,
And a woman can live,
Just for the cut of a cake,
Yet here, that's not the case.
These two have found true love,
In each other, and in their God above.

My Tour

I took Highway Five,
North through California and Oregon,
Hours of endless driving,
I captured strange aromas.

The sights and smells I caught,
The northern air refreshing.
Adventures that I sought,
Became quite interesting.

Mount Shasta smiled at me,
I sat down at her feet.
The city that bears her name,
Had grass, green and neat.

I saw a big blue lake,
Below a mountain high,
Passed many towns on my way,
And drove on, by and by.

A Chinese Plate
(For Chin and Nancy, my Chinese Friends)

I think I'll look for that place,
In Minneapolis, further up the street,
Find out if they're still open late,
Selling delicious things to eat.

I'd like to drive up there,
And order lots of food,
That restaurant is not far from here,
And I know I'm in the mood.

A Chinese plate,
Chow Mein, Wings, Curry Chicken,
Like the time at another place,
I ate almost an entire Asian kitchen.

Oh, I'd like to sit upon a chair,
With food in front of me,
With not a single care,
But for a meal and lots of Asian tea.

Dead Mountain Echo

*D*ead Mountain Echo,"
   Calls to me,
In this town where I go.
I get one for free!
Down deep,
In the Willamette Valley.
Here, moments are measured by secrets kept,
For one mysterious story's told.
Despite the dark clouds this way,
Above the distant pines,
At least once on each Oakridge day,
The glorious sun will shine.

I stand tall,
 On this evening late,
Here, where the town's only light,
Stops traffic on Highway Fifty-eight.
I hear the engines roar,
The noises echo back from mountains high.
It's time to end my tour,
Below the darkened sky.
The light changes to green,
And I begin to walk,
But stop to buy ice cream,

And with Tina talk.

Tina smiles at me,
We stand on the overpass.
If only time allows,
I'll see the sun at last,
Or walk back to the 'Main',
And find something more to eat.
But oh, the noisy trains,
Beneath my weary feet.
Then blue eyes look back at me,
The dark clouds drift away,
And the setting sun I see.
This once it shines today.

Tina and I walk further down the street,
A Chinese restaurant is here.
We eat, we talk with the lovely host,
As end of day draws near,
And I must say good-bye.
Farewell to this tiny town,
Its mountains high,
Where water from the rains run down,
Brings music to my ear.
And eighteen-wheelers come and go,
And oh, what heavy loads they bear.
I stop, I read *Dead Mountain Echo*.

Tina waves a hand at me,

I wave back a hand at her
From where I stand.
I'm in a kind of conscious shock.
My time in Oakridge ends,
And I must leave behind,
My newest friend.
But Tina will stay on my mind,
Though she walks away.
Her pace is slow, I contemplate.
I look, I find my page.
Again, I read *Dead Mountain Echo*.

Oakridge Scenes

T he wind blows straight-line down the path,
    Here in Oakridge where I walk,
The busy engine buzzes late,
For here runs highway Fifty-Eight.

The Cascade Mountains, lofty near,
A sign of strength to quell my fear,
The people dwell near streets below,
The day passes a little slow.

The evening sunsets fade quite late,
Each finds me eating T-bone steak,
But mornings are of essence here,

Hot coffee keeps me awake.

O'er a mountain lives the wind,
As I leave the town the sunset dims,
But Oakridge scenes etched in my mind,
Shall always stay and never decline.

Westport

S pring time in Westport, and the weather is ever so cold.
   At my hotel, I imagine the ocean,
And hear stories told,
Of fish and fishermen,
Of the Atlantic,
The great blue ocean,
And, of granite stones, stacked up like bricks.
One woman asked me, "Man!
Where you are from, do you-all have the stones?"
I answered, "No! No, Madam."
As the wind whipped outside.
The question ensured I'd never forget,
Sir Pinch-a-lot, the blue lobster,
The ocean, and the cold Westport weather.

Westport By The Ocean

W estport!
      Its weather,
Ever so cold.
Mist hangs in the air.
A touch of dampness,
In Spring,
Brings me memories
Of wet seasons in Belize.
For, this little Massachusetts town
And her narrow streets,
Sit deep in a marshy place.

Rock piles are high,
Granite lines the streets.
After sunrise,
A wedding party gathers,
And each other greet.
At that precise moment,
The sky is bright and beautiful,
A priest and a pastor meet,
They greet,
The families and their friends.
The sun is out and brightly shining.

Photographers move around,
Flashing lights to hide the shadows,
Then the music begins,
And in the church, people are seated
But the wedding party stays,
Standing in their places,
Where they line up in formation,
Until the call to order comes.
I see the bride and groom,
Happy and proud in their moment,
One they'll never forget.

Westport stays on my mind,
Like a never-ending scene.
For in that moment,
A couple's dream came true.
In celebration, the reception, the speeches,
The clambake after that. And oh, so funny!
When I stepped outside, a woman asked me,
"Man! In Minnesota, do you-all have the stones?"
"No ma'am," said I,
Perplexed,
And shivering in the cold.

Sir Pinch-A-Lot

In Westport, where the wind whipped,
Like a swinging baseball bat,
On a simple day of sport,
I chanced upon Sir Pinch-A-Lot,
The Big Blue Lobster,
Caged inside a store,
Where crowds of children gathered,
And in laughter roared.
A line wound its way,
Back to where I stood,
Behind Caren and Dave,
My two little friends,
Who stood in line with me,
Waiting to meet face to face,
The one at which we stared,
In that gloomy place,
Where Sir Pinch-A-Lot was kept,
Imprisoned by a human being,
And where he wept,
Confined to a common water tank.

It seemed a mysterious morning,
For the sun was dimly shining,
And outside the wind blew cold,

But I followed the courtesy rule.
Stand firm in the queue,
And wait there on the spot,
For that's what one must do,
If he's to see Sir Pinch-A Lot.
And when the children were through,
Have had their glance
I'd get my chance,
The adults being but a few.
So, my way I made,
As the line wound down to me,
 I pondered the pains I paid,
That blue lobster to see.
As his claws clicked open,
Under a dimming light,
I thought, perhaps, he planned to start a fight,
When the time is right.

My turn came to approach,
Caren and Dave had gone ahead,
And left me queued up in the line.
Then a child's voice announced,
As she pointed to the tank:
"There he is, there is Sir Pinch-A-Lot."
I broke rank,
Moved up close,
And closer still,
Standing taller than the kids,
While others rushed to fill,
That vacuum in the queue,

Wherein I had stood for half-an-hour,
In that gloomy Westport store,
That had made Sir Pinch-A-Lot so bitter,
On that Day of Sport,
When all of us were gathered,
Despite the busy store,
Waiting in a curious manner,
While conversations soured.

One glimpse of that blue fellow,
Revealed his misery and fear,
I wondered why I'd even bothered,
Cause my eyes welled up with tears.
For it was true what I'd heard,
That Sir Pinch-A-Lot was beautiful,
Even in the manner, in which he looked at you,
And clicked his claws together.
But who could ever imagine,
Being taken away from one's home,
And put into a place so foreign,
A gloomy grocery store.
For Sir Pinch-A-Lot was taken,
Out of the ocean deep,
Kidnapped by a human being,
While in a solemn sleep.
Outside the store the wind was raging,
Still whipping like a swinging baseball bat.
Inside, I stood face to face with him,
And saluted the brave Sir Pinch-A-Lot.

City Lights

I made a trip to Chicago,
My first, Fall 1989.
Didn't know what else was on my mind,
Just the city lights.

I grew up in the country,
With the moon shining brightly.
There was no streetlight,
Electricity was not in sight.

These days I still go down to Chicago,
To see my friends,
To feel the Lake Shore wind blow,
And visit museums.

No more do I go just to see the city lights,
As on that fall night in 1989.
These days,
Other things are on my mind.

My Journey

I 've seen Belize's barrier reef,
I've heard its roaring sounds.
I've seen the Maya Mountains,
Blue with an azure mist.

I've seen Guatemala's Lake Atitlan,
Where the Maya people live.
I've seen the Canadian Rockies,
Towering above Lake Louise.

I've felt the coldest winters,
That come in from the north,
Said goodbye to my Mother,
While she was still on Earth.

I've lived in Minnesota,
A land of snow and ice.
I've seen Lake Superior,
And drove the North Shore twice.

I've seen the Oregon coast,
Where a lonesome lighthouse stood.
I've seen Mexico's Mount Orizaba,

Its peak a blanket of snow.

My journey is not over,
Though Mom you've left me now,
I'll see the Andean Mountains,
I'll feel the African sun.

Canada

The summer flowers are blooming here in Canada,
   This is a place of natural beauty.
Once again, I'm roaming deep,
Into towns, cities, and provinces,
As I've moved around from Manitoba,
To Saskatchewan, and beyond.
A much younger man then,
And less wise than I am now.
For through the years,
I've grown wiser, though more forgetful,
Which clearly shows in such a moment as this,
When I write,
And my mind searches my memory,
For an experience,
Long left lodged somewhere,
Down deep in my psyche.

So today I manage to recall,

Not all,
But a few people, places, and things.
Moments great and small,
Like the time when I joined my friends,
On a trip to Calgary.
There was not one hotel,
With vacancy.
The city, a throng of people,
There to see the stampede.
And oh, the hustle,
As we searched for a place to stay.
Today, I still recall the excitement,
The moment I first saw the City of Calgary,
An experience
I shall never forget.

I recall my visit to a reserve,
Like a Native American Reservation,
A short lecture I incurred upon myself,
When I addressed a native man as 'Indian'.
He told me he was sorry,
But I'd made a common mistake,
For he is not an 'Indian,' but an 'Aborigine'.
Then he looked away.
And, I remember the Amethyst mine,
In the province of Ontario,
Where I dug up precious stones,
And was excited there to go,
Though the days were long,
And the roads unending.

I traveled through,
Beautiful forests and little towns.

One day found me in Saskatoon, Saskatchewan,
In the height of summertime,
Practicing to perfect my pronunciation,
Of the name of the city,
The place where I'd remain longest,
And where I met,
A witty, elderly gentleman,
Set in his ways, up in a senior home.
"Hans" asked me up for coffee and a talk,
Then he proceeded to pick my brain,
Unveil my thoughts,
During long conversations.
We discussed the good times in life we had,
And Hans' life when he was young,
We talked about politics–the good and the awfully bad,
While I periodically glanced down at the city streets.

Saskatoon!
This city is so unlike Calgary,
And Edmonton.
Much smaller than both, I thought,
Though my moments there were still as great,
As when a lunch-hour found me on an outdoor bench,
And I had a chance to meditate,
While watching the Saskatchewan River,
Slowly drifting by,
As if on its way to nowhere in particular.

Its water reflected the blue sky,
While drifting past the university,
And now I can still feel,
The peaceful moment inspired by the river,
As a kind of reverence engulfed me.

The long summer was ending,
Limiting my time left to tour,
And I had so much to do,
And more.
We cut through the Rocky Mountain Range,
Went into British Columbia,
And Alberta.
We made a stop at Lake Louise,
Where the sunrise
Lit the moment with colorful rays,
While Lake Louise reflected,
A mirror of the mountain range,
Leaving me longing for another chance,
To see Canada again,
Like I'd seen Lake Atitlan in Guatemala,
And the ancient Maya city of Tikal.

To A Pilot On A Stormy Night

Fly me safely far and wide,
  Fly me down to town,
Fly me towards my beautiful bride,
Fly me faithfully on.

Fly me down below these storms,
Fly me down below,
Fly me where nothing can harm,
Fly me far from woe.

Fly me safely on to love,
Fly me where this plane can land,
Fly me like a gentle dove,
Fly me where life's safe and sound.

Village Wok Nights

S ummer nights come to life,
On the University of Minnesota Campus,
When students stay up late at night,
As if by rule they must.

Chinese food served up at the Village Wok,
This restaurant caters to you.
Students sit in late and talk,
It stays open each morning until two.

Folks drift in off the lighted streets,
Blacks, Latinos, Mixed- races, Whites.
This is where on Summer nights they meet,
And greet each other late.

Sip from cups of Asian tea,
Hot as the summer nights,
Enjoy the chatter of those
Who make your dining bright.

See beautiful women,
Dining beside their friends,
With sparkling eyes and elegant smiles,
They delight the nearby men.

Summer here is like a time for playing,
When students have their fun,
Delicious food served up at the Village Wok,
Dine in, take out, or eat on the run.

BOOK FIVE

WORK WOES AND WONDERS

POEMS

The Waiting Game

The waiting game I play again,
   Just as I do at work each day,
Every moment is the same,
And yet, I'm here to stay.

Sometimes, I wait for hours,
Often, I'm alone.
Sometimes, I lose that stubborn will,
That strengthens my weary bones.

At times, the waiting game is played,
In silence as I linger here,
The issues of my life I weigh,
Deep in my heart I ponder.

The waiting game I play again.
I Waste precious moments today,
Anticipating the call for a sale,
What high price I pay.

On Duty

I'm stuck up here in a security booth,
On a corner where streets converge,
And like the winters of Siberia,
The weather is a blizzard of snow.

A blanket of white,
Fell through the night,
And with might the cold wind blows.
I have a battle to fight.

I put on another sweater,
One more layer of protection.
An extra sweater and this little booth,
That's all between me and the weather.

I'm questioning myself,
Asking for one good reason,
Why I do this outdoor work,
And why in the winter season.

I'm stuck here on a corner, an officer,
I feel the fierce wind blow.
My thoughts and emotions are moved,
On this night filled with blowing snow.

On Night Duty

One more lonesome night is here,
    It finds me gazing at the stars.
I'm a Maya King of past,
From top my pyramid I stare.

Just another night on duty,
The grave-yard shift is mine.
I do Security, And
I stand most of the time.

Just another night gazing up at the stars,
Twinkling, they're gazing back at me.
I think about the strange Gulf War,
And a world of sadness I see.

On this lonesome night I sit,
Again, I stare up at the sky,
My mind follows history a bit,
It makes the time fly by.

Just one more lonesome soul I am,
Living in a world so sad,
Some people want to make millions,
I simply want to be glad.

Sales Executives

We were salesmen, Doc and me,
    And it was often said that,
We should never fail to sell,
And earn our daily bread.

We salesmen went to work,
In the harshest of wintertime.
Some wore jacket and tie, others company shirts.
Then we all waited in line.

Salesmen break at dinnertime,
We jumped into cars outside.
We watched the sunset from there,
Or go dine before someone got the call.

Snow piled up high in mounds of whiteness,
Flakes glittered in the evening sun.
We sold nothing on certain nights,
But the conversations were fun.

Long hours hung over waiting time,
Deep discussions ended with a sudden call.
Someone must work on a client's mind,
Present the product and simply be kind.

So it was on each work night,
We all had a plan of attack.
I made a sale to a young female, a lovely white.
Doc made a sale to a woman, a beautiful black.

Who really knew what made a sale?
We were taught what to do,
How to present the product, and how never to fail.
Still some methods worked, while others fell through.

Nothing I said tonight was reaching my client's head,
This one just sat before me and stared.
I saw Doc at his desk, getting all red,
And I knew just what he feared.

Clients were asked for a simple 'yes' or a gentle 'no',
And quickly tonight came a persistent 'no'!
While each client had cookies, and drinks, and more.
Always more!

Tonight, I think of it all,
While I lie here in bed.
There was no sale tonight, but a fall,
All sales pitches fell dead.

We were salesmen, Doc and me.
We worked hard to earn our daily bread.
Sales Executives.
Gosh! That's what our bosses said.

On Losing A Pender

When did my 'pender'[11] become George's?
 After it was posted?
Can a man keep his worth,
When he finds his earnings looted?

When did George achieve my earnings?
After I had made my sale?
Maybe the man is hallucinating,
Like some ordinary, deranged male.

Oh, when did I lose my 'pender'?
When did George take it away?
Sometimes a man must wonder,
Whether George will steal his entire day.

When your friend is stealing,
How can a man protest?
George is in it for the taking,
Not to protect my interest!

---

[11] A 'pender' is a 'pending sale'. The sale is not final until a certain number
 of days has passed as the purchase may be cancelled.

The Layoff

T heir eyes spoke and said everything.
  Everyone was alarmed.
The news would be unsettling,
Then officially we were informed.

We walked the aisles of emptiness,
Many so little knew.
The end might have come to test,
The selfish things we do.

The other employees asked me: "How long?"
"Ten stretched-out years", I said,
"This layoff–I just don't understand,
But we shouldn't lose our heads."

Their eyes spoke,
They said it all, and more.
None of us thinks,
Anyone will be recalled.

The Golf Balls

F ive golf balls sit still,
   On the break room table
And because they have no will,
They remain quite stable.

They can't just bounce,
Or roll away.
And so, they sit,
From day to day.

Someone must have thought,
A good idea to bring them in,
But now they're caught,
Like me, in constant waiting.

If only they could hear,
To them I'd certainly speak,
I'd find out why they're there,
And ask what is it they seek?

But there's just no way,
That I can know their fate.
Not on any chosen day, would I
Find a way to communicate.

Sales Meeting

We gather around a table,
    The managers conduct a meeting,
And when they are ready,
They'll give us their greetings.

One word leads to another,
Two lead to a talk.
Sentences are what we'd rather,
But any communication meets the mark.

We discuss what we're doing,
Some salespeople linger around.
Wait for the time to sell,
And a deal might go down.

Now heads are held up high,
All faces wide awake.
Some folks never are shy,
While others no noise will make.

The meeting is over on time,
And each one, their real face shows.
Go look in the mirror, prepare the mind,
Or step outside and feel the Fall wind blow.

The Garbage Man

G lasses wide as the eagle's eyes,
Beard as white as wool,
The garbage man tries,
Each day to keep this place clean.

An occasional smile he gives,
An awful lot of talk,
And the little man 'lives',
Near this place where I walk.

Bags of garbage in his hands,
He prances into the meeting room,
As though keeping time with a band,
Playing outdated music and tunes.

He's a friendly little man,
Black suit and dappled yellow tie,
Always lending a helping hand,
But talks too often, why?

Glasses wide as the eagle's eyes,
Sometimes I think of him,
And wonder why
This garbage man is always in.

Though I've not seen him today.
He's seldom gone at noon.
Perhaps, he's on his way,
And will be here very soon.

Farewell Dear Friend
(For Barb)

F arewell, dear friend of mine,
  I think you'll do just fine.
We've worked together long,
And sung our friendship song.

Each Friday I shall think of you,
When there's little work to do,
But if the day is hard,
I'll silently whisper–Barb.

Go on to the shift you chose,
It will not be a beautiful rose,
But things grow nicer every day,
And on your new shift, life could be that way.

Remember not to break too soon,
And don't bring food into the room.
On the old shift you had your fill,
That might not fly on top of the hill.

We might not meet each other now,
But if you see me, take a bow.
I wish you all the best today,
And may that shift turn out okay.

Another Day

Another day at the office,
Another day drifting by,
On my way to nowhere,
Days passing on the fly.

Another day at the work site,
Another day that will just pass.
I shall get my task done right,
While counting the daily cost.

Another day I'm working,
Another day I humbly live.
Another day I make new plans,
Another day to the boss, I give.

Another day I pull my weight,
Another day at the office I toil,
Another day could help make me successful,
Although success might take a while

Snow Plowing

P lowing snow in a parking lot,
   This was something I'd never done before,
Then one fine morning at work,
I decided to have some fun outdoor.

The first thing I saw,
My boss was using his SUV.
He plowed it into a snowbank,
Then almost into me.

I thought, indeed,
He is gone totally crazy!
Then he almost hit the curb, and a tree.
His windshield had gone hazy.

I watched with some soft glee,
Before I turned my wheel,
Then let my SUV go free.
I felt it slide, reel, and careen.

I rammed it into a pile of snow,
And almost into a curb,
Then I put it in 4-wheel-drive-low,
And heard somebody said "Lord".

I looked behind me to see,
Fred's new, black truck moving.
Old Fred never one to be grooving,
But now unusually indulging.

He put that 'baby' into a lower gear,
It must have hurt his humble heart,
For Fred was never one who could bear,
A spot on his truck, worst it being torn apart.

Never one to bear,
His truck unwashed,
Were a bug to sit, he'd shout: "Gosh!"
Then apply a wash, wax, and polish.

Well, somehow that morning was different.
We were all acting crazy.
Wintry jet-streams and currents,
Made brains hazy.

The temperature fell below zero,
One or two or three degrees.
The cold was being felt,
No matter the fun and glee.

That was my day of plowing parking lot snow,
But we didn't get much done.
I saw the real snowplows approaching,
And that ended the snow plowing fun.

Farewell To Work Tonight

Farewell to my sales job tonight,
    I did my best, I tried.
And it was quite an interchange,
Because my clients lied.

But it's over now,
My first night on the job.
And I'm feeling *kinda* right,
Though not as upbeat as I should.

Still there's a silver lining,
There's more to life than gold.
At half-time, I thought of dinner,
Found that *Old Country Buffet* was near.

My friend Cal and I,
We sat feasting on the food,
Drinking tea and coffee too.
We had no time to brood.

We liked it very much,
The whole first day was fine.
The tours we sold were not many,
But *gosh*, did we ever dine.

Hot Food For Jeb

C orn tortillas baked brown,
  Prepared in the kitchen of the "La Hacienda",
There, young Latina girls walked around,
They smiled, while they collected the orders.

I asked for a burrito,
Two tamales, and refried beans.
Jeb said: "Those will do!"
He felt hungry and mean.

I took the 'take-out plates,'
Para llevar, the sign said,
One for the man, Jeb,
The other for me.

"Here. Take your food,"
I said, to-
The man with big eyes and shiny head.
But he sneered at it.

He took the pepper cup,
Spread its contents all over the food,
But I didn't interrupt,
Though the action seemed quite crude.

We drove back to the workplace,
I went into the lunchroom.
Jeb went somewhere else,
Said he'd be there soon.

I can still hear the scream,
"Where's that fellow?
He's big and mean.
This food is appalling!"

Jeb soon found me happily eating,
And I quickly explained,
How it came to be, that-
He got heat in his brain.

But he continued to glower,
For he'd peppered himself quite well,
Burnt his mouth, burnt his hands,
Burnt his eyes, which were still red.

He rubbed his bald head,
Threw up his hands,
But I ignored old Jeb,
Who acted as if he was almost dead.

On Certain Days

On certain days, crowned with cool,
Candid, uncomplicated conversations,
We followed the simple rule at work,
During thoughtful discussions.

Meeting is usually called to order,
To talk, or simply to make,
Some comments to one another,
About performances to date.

Men listen eagerly,
Along with the ladies that be,
We blend the weak with the strong,
And keep the air feeling free.

The meeting is over, the time comes at last,
The moment to move the product,
When each one makes his pitch.
Some sell slowly, others quickly.

Don't hold your table too long,
Don't speak when a manager talks,
You could be awfully wrong,
And you could put out the spark.

It's important to keep,
The glitter in their eyes,
Make them eager to grab your product,
A piece of Timeshare.

The Refrigerator

The refrigerator at work, they say,
   Will be cleaned out on Fridays.
The cleaners will get rid of alligators, old sandwiches,
All things that can be thrown away.

They say that some people have seen,
Snakes sliding around in there,
Smelled stale refried beans,
And glimpsed a big black bear.

The refrigerator!
Well, what can one believe?
The alligators?
That one I cannot buy.

But it's true,
The old thing often stinks,
With the smell of rats and skunks,
That's what the cleaners think.

Another Day In Sales

Another day has come for me,
Another moment, a minute to think,
To sit and feel another sea,
Of endless links of reason,
Of thoughts afloat inside my head,
Where memories charm the mind,
Where with whispering words they wed,
And glorious ideas they find.

Another day I sit inside this room,
Sometimes, I stand outside to view,
In each week, a night or two,
A half-shaped moon, or a nighttime scene.
Another day brings falling snow,
Another day I sit and wait,
Another day the cold winds blow,
While my thoughts I regulate.

To A Woman At My Checkpoint

H ere you are again,
A lovely lilac in the spring.
Your smile shows joy,
Your thoughts I cannot imagine.

Here you are again,
Eyes as beautiful as spring.
They're so bright,
And oh, what joy they bring.

Here you are again,
The fragrance of spring today.
The freshness of early rain,
Each time you come this way.

Here you are again,
Like a lilac blooming.
Earrings and chains,
Your bangles glittering.

Here you are again,
Radiant as the rising sun.
While the world screams pain,
You seem to be having fun.

BOOK SIX

LAMENTATIONS

POEMS

Questions

Today I stopped in thought,
This day was like no other.
Motionless, I contemplated.
And my thoughts I gathered,
At a place deep in my mind,
A place I seldom entered.

I was in deep thought,
I pondered the way of life and death.
The way death stops the human heart,
The way it takes away one's breath.
And as a life would start,
So, it grows until this fate is met.

On these facts I reflected.
Great questions raked my mind,
Like, why must people grow ever older?
Will answers come with time?
Among the mysteries I pondered,
Why, I find, I fear not death but life.

It helps me that I think things through,
That I ponder the ways of life and death.
And in deep thoughts I recollect,
That nothing lives forever.

Not the great sun, nor the moon, nor the most brilliant stars,
And this frightening thought, makes me wonder on.

Outstanding
(For Mothers Everywhere)

Outstanding are you, Dear Mother,
In your own modest way,
As your world moves on,
From day to painful day.

The elegant throw of your chin,
Upwards,
Still remains
Throughout this day of testing.

This trouble is thrust upon you,
By some unlucky mischance.
A change that brings no good,
But only takes away.

This illness takes away your strength,
Fights against your persistent hope,
Attacks your body,
Even as you try to cope.

Still am here with you,

Your hair all gone,
And while I ponder that awful change,
I cannot help myself; for you I weep.

For you are my *Special Joy*,
The only Mother I have left.
 Outstanding are you, Dear Bettie,
You were and still are The Best.

The Future

T he world's full of failure,
 I wonder what life holds,
There's but little pleasure,
In not knowing what the future holds.

There's failure in our future,
When thinking ceases to be,
And we lose our fragrance,
Like a decomposed pine tree.

Good thoughts are failure's defeat,
We must think our future through,
For failure man does oft repeat,
When good thinking he neglects to do.

The Princess Passes

Tonight, my fight is full of failure,
Tonight, my Fall winds blow,
Tonight, a Father's Faith is furled,
Tonight, disheveled feelings flow.

Tonight, my time is tainted,
Tonight, their world proceeds,
Tonight, the teachers keep their thoughts,
Tonight, the tailors will not sew.

Tonight, the people carry through,
Tonight, the Pope will pray.
Tonight, the paupers ponder life,
Tonight, the two princes will not play.

Tonight, there'll be no laughter,
Tonight, there'll be no gain,
Tonight, there'll be much weeping,
Tonight, I'll feel Diana's pain.

Remembering Goree Island

G oree Island stands,
    Still speaking in the light,
With a strong voice,
She tells the tale of Africa's plight.

There on the Western coast of Senegal,
The blood of slaves wrote history,
And walls recorded reverberating sounds,
The groaning of African people in captivity.

My mind surveys this place.
My body feels the wrongs I see.
The cruel treatment,
Of the people who gave birth to me.

The prison cells are still there,
Where they retain the painful sounds,
And the agony of black Africa,
A continent held prisoner there.

At Goree Island, the white slave traders,
Treated their dogs better than the slaves.
And no one rescued my ancestors,
Not a Christian, not a Muslin, not a Jew.

But through the door of 'no return',
Each man, woman, and child passed out of Africa,
Some to live but more to die, in that overlooked holocaust,
In this Land of Freedom called America.

And now that the history is written,
The pain, the anguish, the wrongs can never be erased.
No! not from the cells, nor the seas, nor the memory,
Of those whose ancestors passed through Goree Island.

Poverty Stricken

How did he come to that place,
A position of endless despair?
He could have asked himself *what*?
Or *how much*? can one -person bear.

Now he finds himself poor,
Without love or money,
Gone are the great feelings he felt,
When days were warm and sunny.

Despair is despotic,
It rules over one's soul.
Not to grow old in poverty,
One must be courageous and bold.

He reached back in time,
Searched through his stock of dusty files.
For in those memories he might find,
Something to motivate his mind.

Battles long fought and won,
He must fight them all over again.
And nothing in life is ever completely done,
For one may have to do it all over again.

Happy Birthday

I 've turned forty- five,
But I entertain no celebration,
Not even slight rejoicing.
Life's too fast.

And there's woe,
That holds my heart,
Though no enduring hardship.
It is all in my thoughts.

I'm never sad,
When I reflect upon my life.
I hope to live much longer,
Not one score years, but twice.

A quarter century gone,
Since my best friend died.
Yet I've lived to be thirty, forty,
And now forty-five.

For You I Weep

You Sucker, still for you I weep!
 I watched you go,
Up toward the open sky,
Or was it deep down below?

God alone knows your confession.
May the truth still make you free.
In this world we face questions,
Without an answer key.

The tides of youthful strife,
Often recede with time.
But you've stolen sacred lives,
Now your own life you cannot find.

I would wish you a million joys,
At the table of Heaven's evening supper.
But no! I wish that for those sacred lives.
Innocence you've taken, you Sucker.

A Father's Farewell
(For Kim)

I n springtime when wild flowers bloom,
Daughter, I always think of you,
Who left me here so soon.
You chose your native land.

Each time these spring rains come,
I wish you all the best.
Grow strong and smart,
As you face life's greatest tests.

Already, I miss you much,
The occasional fights, the daily play,
The places in my heart you touched,
Oh! Did I ever slumber on the way?

I tried to change your strong-willed mind,
Asked you to be clear-thinking.
Your Father's love to search, to find.
Embrace its true meaning.

For if you knew my heart,
Where my deepest wishes lie,

You'd feel the love within my words,
And put aside your centered thoughts.

You always said, "I love you, Dad",
But what's the use of that.
Unless you'll stop to listen,
And put your life on track.

Farewell to you, my little one,
Farewell the memories that were to be.
I only wanted the *best* for you,
Not a farewell from you to me.

Farewell to you who's left me here,
Farewell my heart, my soul.
Farewell spring flowers growing wild,
You've chosen still to go.

I'll see you again on some sweet day,
Perhaps, on a visit to the countryside.
Or somewhere else along life's way.
But never forget that your Father's love abides.

On Visiting A Sick Friend
(For Horatious)

H ere I am, a smile on my face,
  But I'm weak,
And as I walk down this corridor,
I can hardly speak.

My mind is focused,
On only two things.
A friend on his last,
And what gift I can bring.

Now I enter this place,
The hospital room,
Where my friend has agony all over his face.
He reaches for the clouds, the stars, the moon.

I stop stiff and still,
Silence enduring.
Can't say a word to him who is ill,
My heart overflows with the strangest feelings.

My presence isn't much,
Yet, it's more than words can tell,
Though it cannot touch my sick friend,
And make him well.

So here I am,
And he is there.
Tall I stand by his bed,
Helpless and bare.

How can I start,
To even say that I care.
I try to speak,
But my own words, I fear.

There were things I'd planned to say,
Yet, I've forgotten my list.
Don't know what's wrong today,
But something about me is amiss.

"Hang in there my friend,"
Silently I say: "hope till the end.
A tree cut down will grow again,
And the hand of God will give it water."

That I cannot speak,
Means that he is strong,
And I am weak,
Though this seems so very wrong.

Perhaps, he'll forgive me for being unable to speak.
All through my life, folks saw me as being strong,
But today I am weak.
I am so very weak.

My Secret Place

T here is a place inside my heart,
 A place that no one sees,
Where secrets are kept,
And there my mind is most at ease.

My secrets there no one can find,
No master mind unveils.
Secrets hidden, secrets sealed,
Secrets I choose to conceal.

Many mysteries hidden there,
Just memories kept for me.
My faith, my feelings, my fears,
Hidden from peering eyes.

For that is a place where thieves cannot go,
My secrets safe from woe.
A place where sweet memories are kept,
And where my deepest secrets lie.

Dear Mother

(For My Three Sisters in Minnesota:
Diane, Hortense, and Yvonne)

I fear, I agonize for you, Dear Mother,
Although some folks see me
As a Deserter.
My mind is troubled that I am,
Not strong enough to help you now,
And make you well again.

So broken I am each woeful day,
That sadness falls as tears.
My heart is weighed,
For Illness has befallen you.
And now I pray; what else can I do?
I beg God's healing power.

Just when I thought that life was fine,
As it was in my youth,
Thinking your life would not soon end.
Just when I thought we were too far apart,
And I'd like us to be closer.
Illness has befallen you.

But you show great strength,
While I feel helpless and sad.

Must I accept this as reality?
Oh, how I seek Strength,
I pray as the days go by.
In frustration, I ask God Why?

I lost my hero father,
Next was my biological Mother,
Then it was my friend Arnold.
Yet, I'd never imagine, Dear Bettie,
It would be you, this illness to suffer,
No never, Dear Mother.

Incident

B ut when did it happen?"
I asked a friend.
"It wasn't like him", she said.
"Good Heavens!"

We sat there talking
For a long, long time.
And we pondered,
That past co-worker of mine.

His only hope now is a Life,
Behind prison bars.
Maybe, twice that many years,
If his life is spared.

Little matters now,
For his girl is dead.
One shot in her breast,
And she was put to rest.

She left this land,
Murdered for what he called 'Love'.
Felled by his evil hand,
An abomination.

Gone is she,
And going is he,
Perhaps, to his death.
Or to whatever the sentence will be.

Our Friend

T he friend we knew,
    Would not hurt you,
That's what we thought.
His honest face was what we bought.

We were shocked when the news we heard,
Our friend went mad, a story sad.
The friend so nice,
Had shot his pregnant wife.

The police came,
With guns well aimed.
They fired not,
A noteworthy act.

Our friend was taken, his mind shaken.
He was given a cell,
In it to dwell, and,
There to live out the rest of his hell.

BOOK SEVEN

SPIRITUAL REFELCTIONS

POEMS

The Call

I Was told a Call came from God to me,
It was through a preacher's words,
But I could not answer that Call,
For I did not believe.

I sought the Preacher's counsel,
His solemn words about the Call.
His words still echo in my mind,
Words which now I ponder.

Long hours passed, with days of thought,
Yet, my mind would not accept the Call.
But time would later change my heart,
In prayer, I gave to God my all.

I Seek Absolution

What did I do that was so bad?
 What wrong road taken?
What song did I sing wrong?
What error did I make?
For now, dear God,
I cannot hear Your calling.
Are you a God too Big?
Or are you a God too Small,
To forgive someone like me?
Am I the piece of carpet,
Curled up after use,
Or a crust of dirt under a shoe?
Oh, what winter coldness!

What wrong not right,
What sins have I committed?
What pain they bring,
What did I do,
That I can never
In words tell?
I am not proud, but meek,
Humbly I speak, I ask again.
What did I do wrong?
And now what path do I go down?

What seeks a wayward man?
Dear God, I ask forgiveness,
And seek total absolution.

God

S ome folks speak of God,
And I know a man who says,
"There's no God above,
Who guides man in his ways."

Some folks believe in a power,
Not so much in God.
Others think they don't need Him,
That God doesn't really care.

Some folks believe in Heaven,
They who rely on God.
They pray over food and drink,
They teach that God is Love.

The Day Departs

As day declines,
I cannot find,
The light of God in me.

I search my heart,
As day departs,
How sure the darkness be!

The days of prayer,
When life was fair,
I know no more forever.

My silent years,
Now bring me tears.
My golden dreams are over.

Life's end draws near,
Death's calling here,
I've lived my fullest joy.

And now I fear to face the end,
No joyous bells I hear,
Welcoming me into God's Heaven.

F. Daniel Brackett

The Missionary[12]

I stood in a crowd,
And felt abandoned.
The noises of voices grew loud,
On a lonesome day in Lebanon.
A man was passing through the town,
 Some reason for my thirst.
The moment seemed eternally long,
And my day was getting worse.
Except for me, the world was at his feet.
Not the whole universe,
But my own private world, at least.
Until I was back home in my house.

The crowd surrounded the missionary,
A scene from first century Palestine.
For he too carried a rugged, wooden cross.
Then my mind moved back in time,
My thoughts to the man called Christ.
For, like Him, that man had stopped to rest,
He gasped for air with all his might,
As if to mimic the Nazarene.
I stood there burdened with my sins,

---

[12] Based on a story told to the Author by Arthur Blessitt

Till I decided to seek relief,
I thought by touching the missionary,
If only I could reach his feet.

Too late it was for me,
That man soon left the Middle East,
I'd missed my only chance you see,
Wasted effort at my finding peace.
But the savior of all things is time,
It can calm the turmoil in one's heart.
I put that man out of my mind,
Towards my future made a start.
The years went by,
While I travelled on with time,
Around the world I went.
Much like that man I'd seen in Palestine.

Time can take a man down or it can lift him high,
It has prolonged my lonesome life,
But seeing that man had lit a fire in me,
And it was still burning bright.
I settled down in Belize,
With little memory of the past.
But one day I looked up from my chair,
Then I saw that man and his wooden cross.
Memory makes up many lies,
The mind might play tricks on a fellow.
At times, one may not believe his eyes,
Yet, I knew I'd seen that man before.

"Come, sir, let me pray with you,
Kneel at your feet today."
The words fell fast from my mouth.
"I've waited years for you to pass my way,
Ever since I missed you in Lebanon that day."
I knew that man was not the Christ,
Yet, some time ago he'd touched my life,
And now, at last, much more today.
Though I might not see him again,
Oh, what joy he'd brought this way,
Despite his journeys and his fame,
He'd stopped and called my name.

Sacred Days

A ll days are for God above,
   He gives me life and peace,
Days for the God of Love,
When at His table I feast.

All days are for worshipping,
The God who gave me life.
Days aren't just for living,
All days I give to Christ.

All days are for the Omnipotent,

He who sends down rain,
Good spiritual fulfillment,
That takes away life's pain.

All days are for the Master,
The greatest God of all.
He who crushes evil actors,
And makes the arrogant fall.

God's Call

Y ou are Called by God,
    These words were often said.
So, I began to think,
With a sober head.

The Call was all I needed to hear,
The summons I'd come to know.
Either one was God's friend,
Or he was God's foe.

That is what the preacher said,
But he convinced me not that day,
Wasted time spent,
That was my youthful way.

Yet soon I received the call, I found religion,

The way to Heaven's shore.
I took that preacher's invitation,
Entered the church's door.

Twenty years since I've answered the Call,
And took the Christian vow.
Still, I hear that preacher's voice,
His message? I rethink it now.

Star Of Heaven

S tar of Heaven,
Look down on Earth,
The life you've given,
What is it worth?

A few short years,
And the human body wears,
With blinding eyes, and deafening ears,
On Earth You give no guarantees.

We have much life at birth,
In youthful days
There's joy on Earth.
But You do things in bewildering ways.

So, Star of Heaven,
Look down on me,
Touch my sick body
And let it be free.

Listen

L isten to the sounds of bells,
   They're ringing,
Somewhere in a place,
A home called Heaven.
The Angels there are waiting.
They've opened the gates,
And came down the stairs,
Of the city of Heaven,
Where Saints can enter in,
And the Blessed can follow.
Should I go ahead,
For You, I will prepare.

I hear the joyful bells,
And I see Arnold like an Angel there.
He is ringing them,
Before my very eyes.
Arnold's ringing, singing,
And I didn't even know
That he could sing.

So sweet is one's song
When not to Earth bound.
Towards Heaven's gate,
By Faith, I journey on.

Where

Everyone journeys down this way,
On a road towards decline.
A constant hurl through this fragile world,
Then comes the end of his time.

Where do we go at the end of life?
What do we do in our new home?
Who can tell what's in the beyond?
The place of the Dead is still unknown.

We speak of Heaven, Hell, and other places,
Where some say the Dead will live again,
In lasting peace or in everlasting consequences,
For Death may bring sunshine, or fire, or rain.

The Greatest Angel

God can be seen as the Greatest Angel,
   With wings that bridge Heaven and Earth,
From one end to the other.
Strong wings,
As an eagle's wings, but stronger,
And far reaching.
Availed in flying here and there,
Where humans await an Angel,
In time of need.
Because of illness or sadness,
Or even madness,
Hurts to the body,
And sometimes to the soul.
One cries out for God to come,
To aid him or her in this earthly hell,
Where there is yearning for His help,
For God is the Greatest Angel of all.

A Child's Prayer

Oh Eternal Father!
　　You are bigger than this day,
So please protect this little flower,
As I bloom along life's way.

You're like a giant gardener,
Stepping between young plants.
I'm a powerless child,
In an endless world of wants.

So Eternal Father,
As you do your daily work,
Keep your eyes upon this flower,
And tend me with your greatest Love.

On His Last Days

I heard that Pope Benedict XVI,
Went back home today,
The last moments of his life to live,
In Regensburg, in a familiar way.

The Pope went home to live,
And pass his final days on Earth,
To put at ease his mind,
In the place of his birth.

I think that God will bless him,
While the Pope is in that place,
His solemn soul will be at peace,
Until the end of life's long race.

But what shall I now say,
About His holiness?
Or what more shall I pray today
When before our God I kneel?

I wish him well,
While his time on Earth is passed,
Days before the Angels toll eternal bells,
And he is in Heaven, at last.

BOOK EIGHT
ANTHOLOGY

POEMS

Eeny, Meeny, Me No More

E eny, meeny, miny, moe,
Your tongue is smacking to and fro,
So put your feet inside your mouth,
Or you will eat my big black toe.
Eeny, meeny, I won't say more.

Epigram

I hate the darkness,
But I love the light.
In the morning when I rise,
I like things bright!
Give me the sunlit days,
And you take the dark, dark nights.

I'm A-Sailing

I'm a-sailing on to places,
Sailing on the sea of life.
I'm a-sailing on to places,
But each day a battle I fight.

Songs For Christmas

Christmas Carols a-coming,
Songs so sweet to hear.
Some folks will be singing,
With voices loud and clear.

The bells are already ringing,
The carolers will sing with glee.
For Christmas is a-coming,
To make our spirit free.

No song will be left to chances,
No melody too sweet,
No soul will sit in silence,
When Christmas Carolers meet.

Halloween

With new faces and costumes,
　　As if the north wind does not blow,
Some dress with the faces of animals,
Others go with the flow.

The new faces are everywhere,
Ghost, not women and men,
Are here to party,
Till Halloween comes to an end?

There's no messing around,
No fuss, just the usual fun,
As this social thing goes down,
From evening 'till the morning sun.

Drinks are not free, no not yet,
But next year, hopefully, they might be.
Still, we don't sigh or break a sweat,
We just pat a possum on the back.

It's Halloween and I can see it now,
Am just waiting for the sun,
Laughing a little,
Before the celebration is done.

Life Changes

L ife for me is often like a dream,
When with the weather I walk,
Early in the mornings.
I set myself into a scene.

Life twists and turns and curls,
But in the suns of summer seasons,
It brightens up my world.
I shine, beyond belief.

Life brings either pleasure or pain,
It changes like the weather,
And it always involves rain,
that runs down the birds' feathers.

Life gives us wings,
We didn't know we had.
And like some ancient kings,
We can become quite mad.

I am often like an Emperor of Rome,
my mood changes like the weather I mean.
Today, I feel like a cat, but more like Caligula.
I'll simply go back to bed, and to my sweet dreams.

Live A Full Life

There's a time when life is filled with pleasure,
Our hearts find reasons to sing,
Not a moment's left for silence,
We absorb the joys of living.

There's a time when life is filled with singing,
Our voices trumpet new songs,
Like noisy birds in a distant tree-top,
We rejoice the whole day long.

There's a time when life is filled with giving,
Our hands reach out to the poor,
We give a moment of silence,
To remember departed souls.

There's a time when life is filled with sorrow,
Our pain seems too deep to bear.
We wish for old times of pleasure,
Singing and laughter and joy.

So, let's live life to its fullest.
Drink wines for the joy of the heart,
And if ever we have to suffer,
Prevailing, those joys will never depart.

What's The Use?

W hat's the use?
          This is our question for life.
Oh, the things we abuse,
When we're not doing them right.

Things fall apart
In the midst of a perfect run,
And we'd better not start,
Unless the right things will be done.

Completion is a must,
Even if questions remain.
Instead of trashing, let's try,
And in doing good we might gain.

Oh, the things we abuse,
The question we asked.
What's the use?
We won't even build the box.

When I Write

I am troubled in body,
Frustrated in mind,
Sad in silence,
Joy is not necessarily mine.

When I write, I am not tolerant,
Of anyone who intrudes,
Who asks questions,
Or tries to get my attention.

When I write, I sit down,
Somewhat like a god,
And attempt to commit,
An act of creation.

The Pen

The pen is proven in its place,
It traces, prints, and writes cursive.
A journalist not writing in haste,
Can make the pen explosive.

The pen has made a mark through history,
Its ink has flowed through fiction.
With the pen, writers in their inventiveness,
Have ignited the world's imagination.

The pen is small but great,
Its uses make men free,
I once wrote with lead on slate,
Before the glorious pen came to me.

Today the pen is being avoided,
Some writers push for speed.
Computers are appearing,
They're faster than the pen can be.

The pen will prove its power,
Its ink will grace more sheets.
The pen will still work for writers,
When computers overheat.

The Creator

I 'm the creator of lines,
I use rhythms,
And rhymes.
I write to comfort the living.

I create lines for humans,
Caught up in the stresses of life,
Hardships, incidents,
Wrongs instead of rights.

I'm the creator of rhythms,
Rolling down on pages,
Fighting life's fears and misgivings,
And the difficulties humanity faces.

I'm against anything that brings outcry,
I the creator of lines,
Help to renew past dreams,
And the life that once mattered.

I'm the author, the writer, creator of simple lines.
I write arduously, no magic.
I create tortured rhymes,
They fight life's fears and misgivings.

Words

W ords are agents of thoughts,
    Spoken or written in intended places and rows.
Like streams of water they can flow,
And they can falter.

I, in segmented spaces of time,
In astute places of my mind,
Direct the way a word will fall.
Each responds and reacts to my call.

A word might act to add alliteration to a line,
Others, rhythm and rhyme.
Imagery in a reader's mind,
Or in letters with written lines.

Each word carries at least an idea,
May disseminate fact, fiction, fallacy, faith, or fear.
Some words become agents of pain,
Others of pleasure and treasure.

In time, a word's meaning will never be clear.
Imagine a word, a reason for war.
Then politicians will not seem so clever,
The meaning of many words might change forever.

Read My Sheets

Don't dig too deep,
Don't feel offended.
Don't read my sheets,
If you know you shouldn't.

I write for me,
It's not for you.
For the things you see,
Might seem senseless to you.

But should you read,
Try until you find,
Nuggets in my writing.
That can enlighten your mind.

No wisdom comes,
Unless the heart is seeking.
No river runs,
Where water is not flowing.

So, dig deep,
And you should be thorough.
Some ideas you'll keep,
Some you'll barrow.

The Clock

S o much to do,
So little time.
The ticking clock,
Can blow the mind.

We work, we play,
We hear the clock.
It's scolding tick-tock,
Time to get back.

What can we do,
To stop the clock?
The passing time,
We can't turn back.

Death is a monster,
Precise as the clock.
So much living we do,
So little time before the ticking stops.

The Sculpture

A sculpture?
How seldom,
Do I ever think of one,
Like nature,
Often for granted taken.
But now I do think a little,
About that art-form forsaken,
By me and, who knows,
How many other persons?
As we grow, we oft forget,
The things that we can do,
And abandon the chance,
To shape, to make, and to build,
Or to simply create,
At will.

What's It Worth

What right way would it be,
If we will to be free?
What would life be worth to me,
Without these eyes to see?

What are wishes worth?
We whisper with doubt.
Worry and wonder and wrong,
We willingly waver about.

The weather wildly wavers,
Wishes will always be free.
We whisper wildly.
What wound wells up in me?

Uncommon Vision

Y ou're just another fellow,
In simplicity you live,
Like an ordinary sparrow,
Your life is like a quiz.

When you wake up in the morning,
Tell yourself your plan for life.
You may have some longings,
But your vision's not too bright.

The answer to each quiz is hidden,
Only the wise understand.
To fools are no revelation given,
But you've figured things out right.

The Ordinary

One ordinary man can be,
   One extraordinary soul,
A sail on the Lake of Life,
In his own world, he grows old.

One ordinary guy,
One extraordinary life.
A simple dream taken to the sky,
From the lowest place to towering heights.

One ordinary dream,
Is an extraordinary thing.
It evolves in the heart and mind,
It takes on eagle's wings.

One ordinary man,
An extraordinary situation.
Only a determined faith can bring,
An ordinary man's elevation.

Don't Stop!

Don't stop!
 You must go on,
And make your mark,
While you are young,
And age has not taken you down.
Work the hours long.

Don't stop!
Push on towards the top.
You can climb any mountain high.
For since time begun
Men have always won,
Against obstacles if they tried.

Don't stop now,
Even if you think,
You're old and near the end.
Hold on to a friend,
Assail to ascend,
For you're almost at the top.

So never stop!
Remember that where men have gone,
They've found success.

You're close to the top,
Of the beaten path,
With one more mile to go.

On Voting

P ick your man,
    And put one down,
For one is like the sands of time.
Always downward sliding.

As the wall-clock ticks,
It's ever harder to pick.
So much the one put down may lack,
Exactly that, your man might fix.

Maybe you will not vote,
But that is not the patriotic way.
Let him not go forth, the one put down,
On the next election day.

Before you vote,
Think on what to do.
Act for the whole country,
And give voting some worth.

Go pick your man in this election,
And put that other fellow down.

It's time you take a stand,
Don't vote the way you've always voted.

The Election

T he day has come and voting's done,
   Many surprises there,
One's down, more wars are on,
There's four more years to bear.

So onward we march,
For victory we searched,
But hope is not lost,
We struggle on together.

The other remains,
The White House holds,
But it's no lasting pain,
Each president passes the baton.

Deficit high,
The economy suffers,
Less cash with which to buy,
The middle class ever poorer.

Hail to the ones,
Who voted 'new,'

Don't wash your hands,
Bear these four years through.

On Socialism
(For Pedro)

I'm not a socialist,
Not a part of the plot to kill,
Democracy and the capitalist,
Or engage in a test of wills.

My fight is for Democracy,
I like the right to vote,
The option to live consistently,
In a land of lasting hope.

Go push your Socialism,
Find your place in its coil,
I am for Capitalism,
And the Democracy of the Western World.

Another Day Ends

Little time is left,
After morning slowly slipped away,
From sunrise through noon,
It's now pass midday.

Somehow the sun tells me,
It's too late to carry on,
With the time,
All passed and gone.

The clock is ticking,
Moving like the golden sun,
Inexorably on its way,
Forever, on and on.

Moving towards an unending destination,
Or a brand-new day.
Tomorrow my work will be resumed,
The sun will keep moving on its way.

A Toast
(For Mark)

M an, you're married now,
   And I must give counsel,
To your wife I bow,
But to you, I speak.

Some advice to help you along.
To hear is your choice,
But it's not a 'right',
And it's not a 'wrong'.

Don't be too quick to confront,
You must be a patient man.
Men are often blunt,
Sometimes, we think we're always strong.

Many women wear their emotions,
Be they strong or weak,
And you'll get a commotion,
When stupidly you speak.

I'm here to say,
That you should show love,
For love is the way,
Of God above.

Whatever you do,
Don't hit your wife,
I tell you now,
Resolve not to fight.

Stay by her side,
Be her strong man.
And take much pride,
In being a good husband.

Cause, after all,
What's one's purpose in life?
It is to stand up tall,
By doing what's right.

Live for the greatest good,
No matter what you achieve,
Enjoy your manhood,
Take life with ease.

If you go to church,
Take the family along,
For life is difficult,
When Faith's not around.

These things I've said,
As your Best Man,
Don't wait till I'm dead,
Before you understand.

Go now, my friend,
And walk with the wise.
Be strong till the end,
Happiness your prize.

We live today,
And tomorrow we die.
Choose your path now, and
Live a truth, but don't live a lie.

On Living

L et's look at each other
   With wide opened eyes,
For no matter how difficult
Things used to be,
We did make it to here,
Lived long enough to see
The 21st Century.

Improved technology
Came into being,
Everything from T.V. to P.C.,
Firewire and devices
That need no wire.
Cell phones decreasing in size,
SUVs getting bigger.

The Twenty-First Century!
Who would have thought,
That we were going to see,
By God's Good Grace,
With wide open eyes,
And alive,
The Twenty-First Century.

Visit our website: Fdanielbrackett.com
And at Facebook:
www.facebook.com/fdanielbrackett
Instagram: @fdanielbrackett